Fit t

Sustaining Effective Ministry in a Changing World

Chris Edmondson

DARTON · LONGMAN + TODD

First published in 2002 by
Darton, Longman and Todd Ltd
1 Spencer Court
140–142 Wandsworth High Street
London SW18 4JJ

ISBN 0–232–52431–9

A catalogue record for this book is available from the British Library.

Designed by Sandie Boccacci
Phototypeset in 9.75/13.25pt Palatino
by Intype London Limited
Printed and bound in Great Britain by
The Bath Press, Bath

Fit to Lead

To Susan, Martin and Tim,
my immediate family,
and to the family of St Peter's Church, Shipley.

Contents

Acknowledgements   ix

Preface   xi

1 Taking the temperature –
the context for ministry at the beginning
of the twenty-first century   1

2 Identity and morale   15

3 Taking care of ourselves   29

4 The nearest and dearest   48

5 Who cares for the carers?   73

6 Tools for the trade 1:
personal development   89

7 Tools for the trade 2:
ministerial skills   104

8 Epilogue: time and choice   126

Notes   133

Select bibliography   139

 # Acknowledgements

this book owes its contents to many friends, colleagues and church communities, who have helped me learn about the role of ordained ministry and leadership in a changing world.

I would like to acknowledge the influence of two men in particular – Tom Anscombe, my training incumbent in Huddersfield when I was a young curate, and Father Simon Holden CR, my spiritual director for over twenty years. These men, by their example, support and challenge, mean more to me than words can adequately express.

Thanks are also due to many people who have encouraged me to keep going while writing this book, to those who have allowed me to interview them, and those who have read and commented on the manuscript of the book in its various forms.

Finally, I must acknowledge my debt of gratitude to Andrée Freeman, a colleague in the staff team at St Peter's, Shipley. She has not only typed the manuscript but also, as a training consultant working in the area of personal development, offered much helpful advice along the way.

Preface

he origins of this book are to be found in a conversation I had early in 1999 with my spiritual director, Father Simon Holden CR. After almost 26 years in ordained ministry, with encouragement from both the Diocese of Bradford and St Peter's, Shipley where I was vicar, I was to take a three-month sabbatical in the summer of that year. How would I use the time? While ready to heed advice not to 'substitute one kind of work for another', nonetheless I wanted to have a focus for my reflection and study during that period.

In the course of the conversation with Father Simon, it became clear that he had noticed that I had a growing concern for issues of morale and identity among clergy. This had been developing over a number of years, particularly through my work as Diocesan Officer for Evangelism in Carlisle Diocese, and more recently as Chairman of the Bradford Diocesan Pastoral Committee. The upshot of the discussion was that I decided to explore this at more depth during my sabbatical, and I subsequently visited six Anglican dioceses in England, talking with bishops, Continuing Ministerial Education Officers and others concerned for the pastoral care and ongoing training of the clergy.

The first fruits of that, in written terms, emerged in *Minister – Love Thyself*, a Grove Book published in 2000. The positive responses to this short book in turn led to people suggesting I might write at greater length on the subjects covered there, because they were pertinent to the changing situation in which the Church and its clergy find themselves, at the beginning of a new century. I am grateful to Darton, Longman and Todd for giving me this opportunity now, and to Grove Books for permission to use some of the material from my earlier work.

My aim is to bring together, under the covers of one book, a cluster of issues, challenges, concerns and opportunities that especially face clergy in their leadership roles in a fast changing world. In this context, is it possible to sustain a healthy and effective ministry? I believe it is, but it will require some fresh approaches from the clergy themselves, those who have responsibility for them in their dioceses or the equivalent, and the local church communities of which they are a part, and where they are called to exercise leadership.

Because this book is primarily about the role of the clergy, is it only intended to be read by and applicable to them? As St Paul was wont to say, especially in his Epistle to the Romans: 'By no means!' Of course, I hope it will be particularly helpful and encouraging to serving clergy and those in training. But not least because of my total belief in and commitment to teamwork and collaborative ministry, this is also a book for anyone who is working in a leadership role in partnership with the clergy, or who cares about their morale and well-being. I have long been concerned that the Church invests large sums of money in the education and initial training of clergy but, after ordination or its equivalent, ongoing training and support is often patchy. My conviction, expressed in this book, is that this need not and should not be so.

Obviously, I write from the standpoint of the Anglican Church – the church in which I grew up, in which my own faith has been nurtured, and in which God has called me to serve in ordained ministry. However, although much of my illustrative material reflects this background, my researches and conversations have taken me into many other denominations and streams. I hope therefore that readers from traditions other than Anglican will be able to apply anything relevant to their own context.

As far as terminology is concerned, I am aware that this is a vexed question. Readers will no doubt have their preferred option – priest, minister, pastor, clergyman or clergywoman. I have chosen to use the word 'minister' when referring to an individual, and 'clergy' as the collective noun. Again, please translate any of these terms that jar or seem to be inappropriate.

I write very much as a local church practitioner and my hope and prayer is that by reflecting on the issues raised here and acting on the practical suggestions, those of us in ordained ministry might be better equipped for the long haul – that we might indeed be fit to lead.

1
Taking the temperature –
the context for ministry at the beginning of the twenty-first century

early in 1993, the manufacturers of the board game Cluedo announced that they were considering eliminating the Rev. Green from their list of suspects. The thought was to replace him with an aggressive business executive. In the end this did not happen but, commenting on it, Ian Bunting writes: 'In real life, clergy have rarely been suspected of murder. They have, however, been among the socially significant characters of British society, some of which are numbered among the characters of the popular board game.'[1] Even if 'socially significant' seems an overstatement, clergy have certainly in the past been afforded respect and seen to be of value in society. Now, along with members of other professions and institutions, their role and authority is under question in the emerging society of the twenty-first century. Furthermore, clergy are not seen as essential to the make-up and survival of society, unlike, for example, doctors, teachers or the police. To many if not most people, the clergy and the institution they represent are irrelevant in a fast-changing and apparently post-Christian world.

To illustrate this point further, note the order in Michael Moynagh's research[2] describing a 'list of people to be trusted' in British society today: local doctor; Kelloggs; Cadbury; Heinz; Nescafé; Rowntree; bank; Coca Cola; CHURCH; police; MP. Even allowing for the fact that this survey was conducted before the Dr Harold Shipman scandal came to light in 2000, as a result of which the place of the local doctor may have slipped down the list in some people's judgement, it reveals the extent of the suspicious age in which we find ourselves.

I believe that this change of attitude to people in ordained ministry and to the Church itself has not happened as recently as some would suggest. I was ordained in the Anglican Church in 1973, and my late father was ordained in 1946. While growing up as a child of the vicarage in the 1950s and 1960s and in my own ministry since the early 1970s, I have observed trends which may have accelerated in recent years but that have been discernible for some considerable time. At the heart of these trends two questions emerge, which are key to all that will follow in this book:

> What does it mean to provide leadership in a church that once shaped culture but is now fast becoming, or some would say has become, a minority sub-culture?

> In the light of this, how can clergy find the resources to sustain a healthy life and effective ministry?

In order to try and answer these questions, we need to begin by reminding ourselves of the significance of the changes that have been emerging in society, which in turn affect the context in which Christian ministry and leadership take place.

What's happened to Christendom?

From the fourth century AD when the Roman Emperor Constantine adopted Christianity as the official Imperial religion, until its gradual demise during the past 250–300 years, Christendom was the sacral culture that dominated European society. This was followed by what is described as the modern era, ushered in by the age of Enlightenment and Reason, which in its turn has now been superseded by what is often called the postmodern era, of which more later.

The Christendom era radically changed the way the Church operated in and related to society. From the time of Constantine onwards, Church and State became twin pillars of this 'sacral' culture, each supporting the other. Members of this society were assumed to be Christian by birth, rather than choice, and in most countries church attendance was the norm and marker of that kind of understanding of belonging.

Within this Christendom culture, everyone at least had some awareness of, even if not commitment to, the Christian story. It was a metanarrative which most believed to be true. (A meta-narrative is any 'big story', overarching explanation or philosophy of life, whether Christian, Marxist or capitalist.) Both public and private moralities were deeply affected by the shared beliefs and values of such a culture. In Britain the Church in Christendom mode, in its Anglican form particularly, was at the centre of society. At its best this church offered pastoral care through its clergy, officiating at rites of passage and hallowing state enterprises and occasions, but it also ensured conformity of belief. Such metanarratives are now seen by many as little more than power plays masquerading as truth claims, designed to include the powerful and exclude the weak.

Two examples from the sixteenth and seventeenth centuries respectively, underline the impact and effect of the Christendom model. Richard Hooker (c. 1554–1600), in his *Of the Laws of Ecclesiastical Politie*, published between 1593 and 1662, wrote: 'With us our society is both Church and Commonwealth, and part of them the Church of God, but the self-same people whole and entire.' In other words the church and community are coterminous, leading to the view that everyone has an automatic right to call on the church. In this model, the established church represented the spiritual life of the community, and ministry was identified with the minister.

During the seventeenth century, the priest-poet George

Herbert (1593–1633), who exercised a ministry most notably at Bemerton just outside Salisbury, created a pattern that in many ways has shaped not only Anglican parochial ministry, but expectations of ministry in other traditions too. There were some three hundred people in his parish, and he also had the assistance of two curates. His was a highly personal model of ministry, presupposing a known and knowable community, which, because of society's changes and the decline in numbers of clergy today, is no longer feasible and, many would say, not desirable. But somehow the model and expectations seem to linger on in the minds of both clergy and congregations – even in the nation when a local or national crisis occurs – despite the challenge to Christendom since the eighteenth century.

However, although as John Finney says, 'Christendom, as an overarching cohesive body of belief and morals held to by the great majority of the people in the West is evaporating',[3] evidence of Christendom lingering on can be seen in the preferential treatment still given to Christianity in Britain in a supposedly multicultural, multi-faith society. There is still an established church, the Church of England. There is still government involvement, with the Prime Minister having the final say in the appointment of the Archbishops of Canterbury and York and other diocesan bishops in the Church of England. Certain Anglican parishes are Crown appointments; as I write, twenty-six Anglican bishops sit in the House of Lords, despite discussion going on over the years suggesting that other denominations or members of other faith communities should be represented. Bishop Michael Nazir-Ali writes: 'The Wakeham Commission on the reform of the House of Lords recognises the role of religion in society, and particularly the Church of England. In its proposals it seeks to provide places for the representation of other Churches and other faith-communities, while retaining a significant place for the Church of England.'[4]

Churches of all denominations, along with charitable bodies, continue to enjoy tax advantages in terms of Gift Aid and, before that, deeds of covenant. Furthermore, there are areas in the country, usually more rural in nature, where the Church is still expected to be a major player in community life. The 2001 foot-and-mouth epidemic in Britain showed both the expectations and appreciation of the role of the Church and its clergy, in terms of pastoral and practical support.

Even if it is one voice among many, and undoubtedly increasingly marginalised, the voice of the Church through church leaders, whether at national or local level, is sought on a whole range of matters. This is especially so on moral issues. For example, following the release in 2001 of the two young men who murdered the Liverpool toddler Jamie Bulger in 1993, the Bishop of Liverpool was given many opportunities on TV and in the press to state a Christian perspective on the moral dilemmas posed by their release. When a disaster happens such as a rail or air crash, clergy are not only on hand to help with counselling and appropriate practical support, but are expected to express, via a memorial service or similar public event, the sense of grief or loss felt by the community or nation.

On a national scale, nowhere was this more evident than around the death of Diana, Princess of Wales in August 1997. Much has been written about this but, as one example among many, in a northern city an estimated one-third of the population visited the cathedral during the week following her death, signed books of condolence, lit candles and paused to pray. Similar expressions of grief were repeated right across the nation.

Something akin to this happened following the Dunblane massacre in Scotland in 1996, where sixteen primary-school children and their teacher were gunned down. In addition to the official memorial service which took place there, John Drane, Professor of Practical Theology at Aberdeen University and a prolific author on Church and culture, described how he found a gang of youths aged 17–20 outside the gate of the school where the tragedy had taken place:

> As I watched they took from their pockets sixteen night-lights – one for each dead child – and, kneeling on the damp pavement, arranged them in a circle; then one of them said, 'I suppose somebody should say something.' As they

wondered how to do it, one of them spotted me, identified me as a minister, and called me over with the words, 'You'll know what to say.' Of course, the reality was quite different. As I stood there, tears streaming down my face, I had no idea what to say, or how to say it. Words had not been especially useful to me or anyone else in this crisis. So, we stood, holding on to one another for a moment, and then I said a brief prayer. That was the catalyst that enabled them too to start praying.[5]

Perhaps these examples show that some aspects of Christendom are lingering on after all. The so-called modern era has come and gone, and the Church and clergy may still have more of a role than is often suggested. Perhaps the recognition of this means something is stirring that could be good news for the Church and its leaders, even if that does not always seem the case on the surface.

'Postmodern' and being church

Much has been written in detail elsewhere about postmodernity, but because its existence and effects impinge on every area of life, it is important to consider it as part of 'taking the temperature' – setting the scene for the subject of this book. As to what is meant by 'postmodernity', to attempt to define the word may seem in itself a contradiction in terms, since postmodernity is amorphous and resists any attempt at an all-embracing definition.

Essentially it is a way of describing the collapse of the social, economic and political systems that typified the modernity of the Enlightenment. (The term 'postmodernism', on the other hand, refers to philosophical systems of thinking.) The modern era from the late seventeenth century to the late twentieth century, where reason was paramount and science was increasingly on the throne, saw people putting faith in human progress rather than in God. This new 'modern' world had no need of him. In fact faith in God was seen as foolish and irrational. The Bible was an old book of no relevance to the emerging era, and the Church little more than a gathering of the deluded. The irony to me is that although the Church has in fact operated in the context of a rational modernism for three centuries, it has tried to fight modernism with the weapons of modernism, while at the same time continuing to try to operate with the inherited Christendom model! No wonder there is confusion around and loss of credibility and confidence in the Church and its ministry.

In many ways postmodernity is caught rather than taught; it is less to do with hard facts and more to do with colours of experience. The main co-ordinates are consumerism, electronic networking and globalisation. It is primarily about the medium rather than the message, so in this sense can be better described as a mood rather than a coherent philosophical position or belief system. It was actually Arnold Toynbee who first used the word 'postmodern' in the 1950s (although its origin is generally attributed to Frederico de Oris in the 1930s.) Two world wars, Hiroshima and the Holocaust provoked a powerful reaction against the modern paradigm. Such events severely challenged, not to say undermined, a linear, 'rational' view of society as progressing steadily from the Enlightenment onwards. Events in the world since then have only served to further erode whatever residual optimism was left about human beings and society. J. W. Fowler remarks that 'Many acute observers suggest that presently we are in the midst of a watershed time of cultural and intellectual change that equals or exceeds the eighteenth century Enlightenment in depth and significance.'[6]

Some observers, however, would place the onset of postmodernity much earlier, and cite the philosophy of Nietzsche and the rise of Nihilism as the death knell of Enlightenment rationalism. S. Grenz, for instance, says, 'The publication of [Nietzsche's] *Thus Spake Zarathustra* (1883) spelled the beginning of the end of modernity, and the origination of the gestation period of postmodernity.'[7] The publication of Darwin's *Origins of the Species* in 1859 also had a ground-shaking impact.

Although the gestation continues, the cumulative effect of all these assaults on the legacy of Thomas Aquinas (*Summa Theologica*, 1265–73) for the Catholic Church, and John Calvin (*Institutes of the Christian Religion*, 1536–59) for the Protestant Church, especially in the area of belief and spirituality, has been to undermine, if not erode, much of the centrality of the Judaeo-Christian heritage within Western culture. The onset of postmodernity was a fundamental sea change, challenging as never before the inherited spiritual assumptions that have undergirded Western culture, not least that of our own nation.

Graham Cray writes: 'All the major church traditions in this country have been shaped by Christendom – by an expectation that they have a special right to be heard and that people "ought" to listen to them. Whole strategies of evangelism have been based on residual guilt about not going to church. But we are now one voice among many.'[8]

In his book *Being Human, Being Church*[9] Robert Warren has addressed the consequences of this sea change helpfully, as he speaks of the Church defined in terms of being in 'inherited mode' and in 'emerging mode'. He has two equations to describe this:

the Church in 'inherited mode' = building + priest + stipend;
the Church in 'emerging mode' = community + faith + action.

It is important to say that 'inherited mode' isn't all bad news. At its best, the Church has an excellent track record in its pastoral work and care. Church buildings are focal points, which represent and offer reminders of God to communities. There are outstanding examples of sacrifice, service and compassion through the Church and its clergy. But, Warren goes on to argue, there is something fixed and unwieldy about the model. The leadership is strongly clerical, with suggestions of a provider–client model. There is a focus on church life issues with the danger of disconnection from the world around, bearing in mind we are now in an era when church and society are not coterminous. The Church in 'inherited mode' functions as an organisation rather than a community, and suggests a single way only of being church, i.e., church = building + priest + stipend.

However, the 'emerging' model, with its emphasis on community, faith and action, does seem to resonate with what is happening in twenty-first-century British society. A search for meaning through relationship is clearly evident. Grace Davie has done extensive research on the way in which people are seeking to 'belong before they will believe'.[10] (Much of this is also, I believe, a reaction to the individualism of the 1980s and early 1990s.) John Finney's research[11] on how adults come to faith further underlines this trend. Recent evidence of this need to belong is seen in the development of internet chat rooms, text-messaging on mobile phones and networking with people who share a common mind or interest.

With all this going on, Warren would argue, the emerging Church needs to put high value on generating a lively and open community, as this appeals to the postmodern mindset. Structures need to be light and flexible to enable the true purpose of the Church to be fulfilled. Faith is seen more in terms of a journey of exploration than an assent to fixed formulas. Above all, people want to know not just 'Is it true?' but 'Does it work?' They want to see evidence of faith in action, injustices challenged and compassion expressed in tangible ways.

In the early twenty-first century, we are in reality a 'church in transition'. For the leaders of the Church, ordained and lay, this can be both a great opportunity and a great source of stress and confusion. The challenge is to meet the expectations of those brought up with what has been essentially a 'Christendom' model of being church while at the same time finding a model that is appropriate and relevant to the changing world of post-modernity. Such expectations are partly generational but not exclusively so. Certainly those born from the 1960s onwards have grown up with predominantly postmodern world views. This is normal for them. However, not least through media and technological developments, people of all ages are affected by what is taking place. We can communicate electronically across the world in a matter of minutes. Clergy themselves, spanning different age groups, will bring their own perspectives and expectations.

Back to the future?

So, is there a visible and viable path ahead? Certainly there is no way there could or should be a return to the Christendom model, even if some might want it. We cannot go back to a world where people respected God, the Church and its clergy by virtue of some innate authority, and where the Marxist claim that the Church was an aspect of social control was sadly sometimes true. Furthermore, although reason has in some sense been dethroned in recent years as modernity has been challenged, it remains important and indeed should be seen as a gift of God. We cannot read the Bible as it was read in the fourteenth century; happily we have the insights of scholarly research and relatively recently discovered original texts. Whatever state of flux the Western churches are in, the overriding concern is to develop a 'theology which is grounded in and held accountable to God's revelation in Jesus Christ'.[12] This theology will of course lead to a practice of Christian spirituality that has integrity and meaning within postmodernity. This will require two things if we are not to throw the baby out with the bathwater:

- a sensitive and caring approach when listening to the concerns which motivate postmodern thought;
- the utilisation of postmodern resources to present the Gospel to a postmodern culture.

We have now, in the early twenty-first century, many people who are not sure what to believe, but who want to believe in something or someone. As the saying goes, 'Spirituality is alive and well but of no particular fixed abode'! The earlier illustrations of the death of Diana and the Dunblane massacre give evidence of that. All the same, this reference to 'spirituality' is often more about self-fulfilment and is relativist in nature: 'You tell me your truth and I'll tell you mine', to quote the Manic Street Preachers' song. Nonetheless, a high percentage of people still say they believe in God, and the 2000 Soul of Britain survey carried out by the BBC showed that over 76 per cent of the population admitted to having had a 'religious experience'. This was in fact up by 59 per cent in just over a decade, and by more than 110 per cent compared with 25 years before. What we see around us is not so much atheism but a lack of moorings or reference points.

Mick Brown writes: 'Spirituality has become an all-purpose description of what people feel to be missing from their lives rather than of what they hope to discover.' This spiritual search is 'a symptom of collective uncertainty in an age when the traditional institutions of Church, family and community appear to be breaking down'.[13]

Could this then be a new 'time for God' and thereby for the Church and its leadership? It may be that postmodernity is characterised by 'nothing matters much', 'nothing is definite', 'anything goes', a life lived by hopping from one experience to another. Thus, in the marketing of BMW cars, statements like 'Happiness is not around the next corner. It *is* the next corner' are made. For the postmodern, boredom and the mundane are unacceptable – as the comic-strip character Calvin says: 'Happiness isn't good enough for me. I demand euphoria!' Multiple choice and 'pic'n'mix' are the flavours of life, a meaningless plurality. Nothing is stable, nothing is guaranteed to last – 'live for the moment' is the watchword. All this could on the surface seem to be the antithesis of Christian discipleship and of what the Kingdom of God means.

Nonetheless, if human beings are no longer standing at the centre as the modern era had them, and reason and science are not everything, could there be a vacuum left that is waiting to be filled by God? The dethroning of reason and rationalism in this sense could be good news for the Church, because rationalism holds that every fact must be known, every question answered and all the data be available on all subjects – including God. Although propositional teaching might be out of favour as part of the rejection of authority, and the metanarrative is suspect, storytelling and narrative theology are in. I want to suggest this as one of the key reconnection points.

Postmodernity has a lot to say about story. It sees personal identity as being defined in the unfolding of the story of life. We all have a story by which we live. Every family has a story and traditions, in terms of photographs, videos, stories told and retold. Our TV screens have endless soap operas on offer, which are essentially people listening in on others' life stories, crises and traumas. What is true of individuals, families and communities is also true of nations – we call it history.

Although, as we have observed, the postmodern scene finds metanarratives difficult and many of the philosophical or political metanarratives that have held sway are currently being rejected or discarded, does that in fact leave space for re-engaging with the biblical narrative? Is the Christian community in a good place to fill that vacuum both through its life and its message? I believe the answer is 'yes' – though we must beware of a simplistic approach or the tendency inherent in the earlier modern era to conceive of God's truth in a monolithic way. If people are to embrace the Christian story, they are unlikely to do so in a 'no questions asked' way because of the current suspicion of metanarratives and the questioning of authority. Here one of the insights of postmodernism comes in – 'undecid-ability', a favourite word of Jacques Derrida. The essence of undecidability is that the truths of life hover between one thing and another. In reality there is nothing new in this and Jesus' teaching is full of paradoxes such as 'take no thought for tomorrow', but on the other hand 'don't build a tower without counting the cost'. The Christian metanarrative (and it must be affirmed as such) is incomplete, at least on earth – 'we see through a glass darkly' (1 Corinthians 13:12). However, it allows us not only to cope with life but also to make sense of it.

It has to be acknowledged that the Church and its representa-tives have often been guilty of 'trimming' the Gospel to fit human stories and expectations, as in some of the Church of England's uncritical support of the darker aspects of the British Empire in the past. Similarly the churches' failure to see or expose Naziism for what it was in the 1930s reflects this. In local church situ-ations, there is a lot of evidence of people being so wedded to how things have always been or been done that new life and new ways cannot develop. The Gospel story is always above and beyond human traditions and needs to be freed to do its liberating work. This is nothing less than a call for a new apologetic – Christians sharing their stories of encounter with God – rather than the Church bombarding people with schematised dogma.

A further clue to the postmodern world comes again from Derrida's use of the word 'deconstruction'. For him, that meant a dismantling of familiar things, in order to rebuild them in a way that restores their life. This word, sometimes misrepresented as being entirely negative, could actually be a key word for the renewal of the Church and its ministry today.

There is an opportunity for the Church and its ministers to see what is emerging as giving a chance both for rediscovery and fresh discovery. Postmodernity's outlook is generally gloomy. Human nature looks to find hope. Today's scene is not a comfortable place for the Church and its ministry but maybe it is more authentic to our roots. In the light of this, those in leadership in the Church in particular need to know where to look for models and resources, ways of thinking that are freeing and enabling, and sources of support that can help sustain an effective ministry. What follows in the remaining chapters attempts to address at least some of these issues, particularly though not exclusively for those called into ordained leadership roles in the Church.

Before looking ahead, however, it is worth taking one more glance back to the first three centuries of the Christian era. Post-Christendom is clearly not the same as pre-Christendom but, as I have commented earlier, if not a heritage, at least a significant residue remains. It has been noted that Christendom approaches continue to be effective for the over-60s, among whom church attendance is growing; and there are some insights to be gained from the movements that operated on the margins as the transition from pre-Christendom to Christendom took place. In *Recovering the Past*,[14] John Finney suggests that the contemporary, emerging church can learn a lot from the Celtic movement that survived and even thrived on the edge of Europe and developed practices and values different from the then emerging mainstream Christendom churches. The Celtic church challenged status, power and wealth as being inappropriate means to advance the Kingdom of God. The downside of the Christendom model as it developed was the tendency for the Church to be at the centre, with the person of Jesus often left on the margins. Is it possible that post-Christendom may learn from those early pioneers and see the Church daring to live more on the margins, with Jesus and his story restored to the centre? As Stuart Murray writes, 'We have to learn what it means to be a church on the margins rather than at the centre, to operate as a movement rather than an institution, and to become unconventional and surprising rather than predictable.'[15]

In this sense, post-Christendom presents a challenge not only about the form of mission but also about the form of the Church. As in the experience of Joshua and the Israelites preparing to cross the Jordan, so we too 'have not passed this way before' (Joshua 3:4). Of all the denominations in Britain, the Anglican Church of which I am a member is perhaps the least used to operating from the edge, from the margins. Fresh, imaginative leadership will be required and will need resourcing. Doing church differently, seeing it expressed in many diverse forms, will no doubt be messy, and mistakes will be made. But once the opportunities are seized, where the story of Jesus has hitherto been unfamiliar, and in a situation where faith can no longer be assumed, imposed or coerced, we may find rich resources from God and his world on which to draw.

2
Identity and morale

there are two issues in particular that arise out of the changing context in which clergy are called to minister – identity and morale.

Identity

It may be true that the clergy are still public figures and, as we have noted in Chapter 1, there are some expectations from society that persist, but nonetheless the effect of marginalisation on a minister's self-esteem and self-image can be considerable. In fact, in recent years, this is true not only in the wider sense of society's attitudes but also within the Church itself. As a minister, who am I? Am I called to be a pastor, a teacher, an evangelist, an enabler, a manager or a fund-raiser? However I describe myself – minister, priest, pastor – are my energies mainly to be directed to caring for the congregation or the wider community or parish? In the book *Leading, Managing and Ministering*,[1] John Adair suggests that ministers need to be managers 20–30 per cent of the time. Even if that managing is intended as a means to an end, and not the end itself, the call to be more businesslike and efficient can feel threatening to some ministers and downright offensive to others. Most ordained people clearly believe that the task of ministry is primarily about a call and vocation, that meeting point between God's call and our response, our unworthiness and powerlessness and his perfection and power. But how is this calling to be worked out today? What is God looking for from those called into this kind of role?

There is a serious underlying theological issue here. 'Theological', we remember, means 'relating to thought about God'. How God is seen, understood and experienced will affect the way ministry is lived out and practised. From wherever it may have come, an image of a demanding God will lead to a driven, guilt-based ministry, where 'he is never satisfied and therefore I can never stop'. When I do stop, either out of choice or necessity, there remains a restlessness which, if its root is not recognised and dealt with, may lead to complete exhaustion or breakdown. At the opposite extreme is the image of a God who makes no demands, which can lead to a ministry without direction or purpose and with little sense of expectation of seeing God at work. Ministry comes to be seen as being concerned to 'survive as best we can', in some instances maybe even counting the days to retirement.

All this requires those in ordained ministry to ask a key question – what is motivating my work and ministry? It may be a particular view of God, as above, helpful and accurate or otherwise, or perhaps a desire for power, status and success, to be noticed, to become well known. There may be a need constantly to prove self-worth, or a working to the expectations of others, real or imagined, rather than from God's particular call to the individual and the consequent response. I suppose I want to ask: is it inevitable that vocational calling should produce driven women and men, as often seems the case?

There may be other issues coming from Christian history and tradition that affect how we see these issues of identity and morale. In the New Testament there are particular exhortations for leaders to live a Christ-like life (John 21:15–19; Acts 20:28–32) and to follow Christ's example (1 Peter 2:21–25). Ministers are furthermore called to 'guard the truth' (1 Timothy 3:9, 6:20–21 and 2 Timothy 1:14), which has arguably never been more challenging than in the postmodern context, where absolutes of any kind are under threat.

When this is put alongside other biblical images of ministry, which are part of our inheritance and history, for example the notions of 'priest', 'apostle', 'prophet' or 'servant', we have something that is on the one hand helpful and inspirational but on the other hand can place ministers under pressure to live up to certain expectations suggested by these roles. Ministers can find it hard to escape from the effects of these kinds of expectations, even if some of these words and what they seem to convey are foreign to their own particular theological positions.

Whether or not a minister is comfortable with the idea of 'priesthood' and its Old Testament echoes of a sacrificial/mediatorial role, nevertheless, across the different Christian traditions, not just the Roman Catholic or Anglo-Catholic, there are clear expectations about a minister representing God to people and people to God. This is evident in the way some ministers see themselves or are seen by their congregations in some of the Free and new churches. In the Church of England's Thirty-Nine Articles of Religion, Article 26 clearly separates out the efficacy of the priestly work of the Church from the worthiness or otherwise of the minister. However, while this may deal with some of the pressures and expectations at a rational level, it does not necessarily do so at the emotional level.

Alongside these (rightly) high expectations of those called into leadership, it might be helpful to give examples from the biblical tradition which also point out the fallibility and imperfections of those so called – they truly are 'human like us'. Whether that be David as seen in the Bathsheba incident (2 Samuel 11), Elijah feeling suicidal in the wilderness (1 Kings 19:4–9), Peter's denial (Luke 22:54–62) or Paul's defence of his ministry as seen for example in sections of 2 Corinthians 10 and 11, there is much biblical evidence for this side of the story too.

To cite such examples is not to make excuses or suggest a lowering of standards as some kind of sign of accommodation to a changing situation. While the perfection of Christ may some times seem to haunt and pressurise, the gospels also reveal points at which his humanity, in terms of tiredness (John 4:6), anger (albeit righteous) (Mark 11:11–18) and despair (Mark 15:24), was evident. Thankfully the biblical tradition allows us to see the real humanity of Jesus!

Outside the biblical tradition, in the autobiographical writings of Teresa of Avila we see that at times she felt herself to be 'half-crazy', for instance as a result of visions of devils attacking a dead man's body at a funeral, such was the inner turmoil she experienced as part of her call to ministry. Equally, her more positive experience of 'raptures' and visions do not suggest a predictable, healthy, steady, always balanced life and ministry!

Whether it is sixteenth-century Teresa or the twentieth-century Trappist monk Thomas Merton, to quote two examples of people often thought of as spiritual giants in the Christian tradition, there seems to be much evidence of emotional stress which has to be faced in ministry, as well as the sense of great privilege.

Morale

When it comes to the morale of the clergy, there seems to be quite a mixed picture in evidence today. In the year 2000, Professor Michael Rose of Bath University surveyed nearly 35,000 workers to find out what made for job satisfaction. Questions about pay, promotion, job security, relationships with the boss, opportunities to show initiative and the work itself were the main focal points of his research. In terms of overall job satisfaction for the different occupations, clergy came out second at 72 per cent, behind medical secretaries who registered 75 per cent. However, in a separate index in the same survey, when the 'feel-good factor' was measured in terms of the sense of personal value and worth, clergy came 71st in a list that had bus drivers, civil service executive officers, forecourt attendants, farmers, construction workers, people in education and a wide range of other jobs and professions reporting more sense of value at work. All this suggests that the issue of morale is not straightforward.

I would put alongside this some work carried out in the late

1990s by Professor Leslie Francis and Dr William Kay from the Centre of Missionary Studies at the University of Wales, Bangor. Based on 754 replies from 2,570 questionnaires sent to pastors affiliated to the Evangelical Alliance in the UK, it emerged that 53 per cent had thought of leaving the ministry at one time or another because of stress. In addition, 38 per cent described themselves as having frequently felt overwhelmed by the complexity of the pastoral demands they face each day. (One practical outcome of this survey has been the formation of the Care for Pastors Network, which aims to offer clergy feeling such pressures appropriate support, including health checks, discounted holidays and professional counselling.)

There are both *external* and *internal* factors that have a crucial effect on motivation and morale.

External influences on morale

There seem to be a number of influential external factors. One is the geographical and sociological context in which clergy are called to work. From enquiries I made in the rural Anglican Diocese of Hereford in the late 1990s, it seemed that clergy morale was relatively high. Factors such as a pleasant environment, a relatively high commitment to church life, clergy still having more of an obvious role, and some of the effects of postmodernity being slower to catch on, were cited as being significant contributors to this. Similarly, in the Anglican Diocese of Carlisle, which had almost half the total of foot-and-mouth cases in its borders in the 2001 epidemic, many clergy spoke of the positive challenge of new pastoral and mission opportunities particularly in the farming community. Similar experiences were recorded in Devon and throughout Exeter Diocese.

On the other hand, for those working in an inner-city context, it may be harder to maintain morale. You may be familiar with the experience of two clergy in Newcastle and Liverpool whom I know. Between them they have been burgled over eighty times in a ten-year period. The number of clergy who have been physically attacked is on the increase. Having worked in urban, suburban and rural contexts myself, I know it would be naive and incorrect to say that ministering in one is an intrinsically easier option than another. Indeed, a report issued early in 2002 by Leicester University suggests that in rural Somerset, violent crime directed towards the clergy is on the increase. I simply make the point that external factors including geographical location do have a significant effect on morale.

A second influential factor is that all the major denominations are facing life with fewer full-time stipendiary ministers. In a *Church Times* report from 15 June 2001, it was stated that although Methodist membership numbers are falling, the number of churches and circuits remains substantially the same. The article went on to state that the decrease in the number of ministers to oversee this work is, not surprisingly, leading to a growing concern over their stress levels.

In the Anglican Church, the year 2001 saw headline after headline in the national and church press about clergy numbers and finances. In 1961 there were over 12,000 full-time stipendiary clergy; in 1999, the latest available statistics at the time of writing, there were 9,648, down from 9,762 in 1997. There have been increases in the numbers recommended for ordination training in recent years, including for non-stipendiary and ordained local ministry, all of which is positive, but even so it does not make up for the number of clergy who have retired in recent years. In 2002 there were reckoned to be over 6,000 active retired Church of England clergy.

An example from the Roman Catholic Church illustrates the problems it is facing. In the Archdiocese of Liverpool in the 1960s there were 600 priests serving just under 300 churches, and 60 per cent of the Roman Catholic population went to church regularly. By 2001, there were 350 priests serving 225 churches, 20 of whom were being expected to work past seventy-five, the official retirement age. Where even as recently as the 1980s, twenty or more men would be ordained priest each year, in 2001 there were, staggeringly, no ordinations in the Archdiocese. There are all kinds of consequences to these figures. In particular, existing priests are exhausted, churches are being closed for a mixture of financial reasons and lack of manpower, and the seminary at Upholland has been forced to close. Positively, there is some rediscovering of the ministry of the whole people of God, and a number of men over the age of thirty-five are being ordained as permanent deacons; but the overall scenario does not help the morale of existing priests, nor that of their congregations. Looking ahead, the Archdiocese estimates that by 2010 the number of priests could be down to 140, half at least of whom would be serving two parishes.

To return to the Anglican scene, in rural areas in particular clergy are spread even more thinly, often with many churches, sometimes ten or more, for which to be pastorally responsible. Positively, this has given impetus to some exciting and much needed developments in collaborative ministry. However, it calls for a fresh examination of what it means, in Church of England terms, to have 'the cure of souls' in this changing context. Multiple structures have to be maintained, for example in terms of church councils, and people in congregations are expected to pay an ever-increasing amount by the share or quota system to fund local parochial ministry. Not surprisingly, resentment is evident when people feel they are getting less and less 'value for money' with fewer clergy on the ground.

In June 2001, the *Church Times* reported, 'One in three stipendiary clergy posts in Truro Diocese is to be cut over the next ten years.' Effectively this means a reduction from 123 to 83 stipendiary clergy. Even allowing for 'natural wastage', and seeing this as a creative opportunity for new lay training schemes, the effect of such 'downsizing' in the workforce on the morale of existing clergy and those considering ordination can be very damaging. This is clearly not simply a problem for more rural areas, because in July 2001, the Missionary Diocese of Wakefield revealed that they needed to prune 25 posts, lay and ordained, because of a projected deficit of £3/4m. Similarly, the Diocese of Southwark announced it needed to find another £1.5m over a relatively short period of time or 80 ordained and lay posts in the diocese would have to go.

Another aspect of finance that affects the morale of the clergy concerns the energy expended to find the money locally to fund the Church's ministry and mission. Each denomination tackles this differently according to its structures, but many clergy feel themselves to be under more and more pressure as fund-raisers, which takes them away from whatever they perceive to be their primary tasks and priorities.

A further time-consuming pressure can be the church building or buildings for which clergy and congregations are responsible. Many of these, especially in rural areas, can be Grade 1 or 2 listed. Their upkeep and the seeking of funding locally and from external sources can be a huge pressure on minister and congregation and can again feel to be a distraction from the main tasks of what it means to be the Church in this changing world.

Whatever else is on the agenda, central to what it means to be 'church' in any era is the task of mission and evangelism. While, as Chapter 1 has indicated, I believe the current scene provides more opportunities than might at first appear, being a minister in a church which is reported to be declining numerically, either locally, nationally or both, has a massive effect on morale. The Decade of Evangelism in the 1990s saw overall Sunday church attendance decline by up to 20 per cent in real terms. Even if statistics show that some of this is explained by changing patterns of attendance, with people coming less frequently and the core remaining much the same, many clergy experience a sense of failure in their role of leadership, in terms of the call to make disciples and keep them. Like it or not, 'success' and effectiveness in ministry is measured to some extent at least in terms of numerical growth.

In the Church of England, the 1999 Sunday attendance figures may have shown the slowest decline for eight years, but there was still decline. A new method of counting in 2000 meant that a total of 1.3 million were recorded as attending church, compared with 970,000 in 1999. By including weekday services as well as Sunday attendance, it is reckoned that a more accurate picture has now been given. It may be there are some signs of hope and renewal; and anecdotal evidence suggests an increase in 2001 following the effects of the terrorist attacks in the USA on 11 September.

In the light of all this, honesty from the clergy along with support from those in senior leadership positions is crucial, as we seek to understand the effect of these external factors on morale. There has been too much 'papering over of the cracks' and superficial talk about a 'leaner', 'fitter' church.

Privileges and pressures

Alongside the external factors, there are significant internal factors that affect morale, some of which have always been around, though not necessarily acknowledged openly, while others are more specifically related to the current climate.

Ordained ministry has rightly always had at its heart a mix of privilege and pressure. Down the centuries, from the biblical tradition onwards, this is apparent. However, evidence seems to suggest that when an institution and the notions and belief systems that support it evolve in an attempt to accommodate rapid social change, this can and frequently does leave those within that organisation in a role vacuum. In turn, this can call into question their internal values and sense of self-worth.

A key difference between ordained ministry and most other professions that are also seeking to accommodate change is the all-consuming nature of ministry, which is often to do with living 'over the shop' and not having clearly defined hours of work. This can lead to a blurring of boundaries. People in other caring professions have more definite work hours, rotas of being on call and off duty, and usually a safe distance between themselves and those whom they serve. The 24-hour nature of the clergy's role can in addition create conflicts for the minister's family – of which more in Chapter 4. As Mary Anne Coate has put it: 'Their [the clergy's] raw material is the whole of life and not just a part of it.'[2]

Linked to this is the way in which clergy, and to an extent their families, are not private individuals. The issue of their own expectations of themselves can be further complicated by others' expectations of them. For example, if ministers are undergoing a personal faith crisis, or a questioning of their vocation, how can they handle that with integrity while continuing a public ministry? The pressure to model discipleship and encourage others in it is hard enough anyway, never mind when such internal struggles are taking place. To take another scenario, ministers who wish to divorce and remarry or who are struggling with their sexual orientation will be dealing with deep inner conflicts relating to their own sense of call and vocation as well as to others' expectations.

Putting the issue more sharply, does a minister have a right to a private life? In theory of course the answer is 'yes' but the expectations of being a 'special' sort of person, not just in the actual work of ministry but in setting higher standards in one's personal life, can be overwhelming. The reality of ministry involves being asked to bear more than simply being oneself, and that is both a privilege and a pressure. Nevertheless, this representative role, however we understand it theologically, should not be allowed to make clergy deny their essential humanness and its inevitable limitations.

This public/private tension has a particular bearing on Roman Catholic priests. The experience of ordination in that church involves a public acceptance of a role and function, similar in many respects to a marriage. The ordination service mirrors the exchange of vows and promises made before witnesses at a wedding. Ordination in this sense makes public a person's inner conviction of calling through a commitment to service, which is itself highly dependent on external expression within an organisational context. Add to this the fact that Roman Catholic priests are paid very poorly, and what they receive depends on the diocese and local church, and it is not surprising that morale is often low, and as we have already noted there are few new vocations to the priesthood.

Reading so far, some might be tempted to think this is an overstatement of the case, and that in reality the clergy have an easier rather than a harder time of it compared with other professions. Certainly the autonomy at work that many clergy seem to have can appear attractive and is indeed a privilege.

Flexibility in terms of working hours is also something that others would be delighted to have. Furthermore, being a minister seems to offer a fairly protected way of life, more secure than most, with few redundancies in evidence. Historically, in the Church of England and other denominations which have a central organisation, that may have been the case, though many Free and independent churches have long had the power to hire and fire their ministers. In these churches, if the local congregation, elders, deacons or council do not approve of the minister or the message or both, then that could be the end of the story.

However, as the picture I have painted about clergy numbers and finance makes clear, times are changing. No longer is there a guarantee of a job for life. Hitherto in many denominations, provided a minister kept clear of open scandal, an income and housing were guaranteed, even if preferment or promotion did not come along. In contrast, people leaving theological and Bible colleges today may not find an initial post; once ordained it cannot be assumed there will always be an opening for ministry in the future. This has inevitable effects on morale, not least because many clergy under the surface are very vulnerable and can appear to be very defensive. This is evident in the whole debate in the Church of England on the matter of freehold, whereby a clergyman or woman, once instituted and inducted, has a right to stay in a parish until the compulsory retirement age of seventy. Many, myself included, believe this to be an inappropriate privilege for the clergy, as well as sometimes being a cause of immense frustration in the local church. Handling this changing scene needs a lot of internal maturity on the part of the clergy and wisdom on the part of those in authority, in order to deal with it constructively. Sadly, sometimes the very freedom can lead to a blurring in terms of accountability and become a source of confusion and strain.

Feeling the pain

Some years ago, John Sandford in his book *Ministry Burnout*[3] listed nine special difficulties facing those in ministry:

- The job is never finished.
- We don't know if our work has any results.
- The work is repetitive.
- We are constantly having to deal with people's expectations.
- We must work with the same people year in and year out.
- Working with people in need saps our energy.
- Many come not for solid spiritual food but for 'strokes'.
- We often function behind a mask.
- We can become exhausted by failure.

Reflecting on nearly thirty years in ordained ministry within the Church of England, from my own experience and observation of others, I believe this to be a very accurate list in terms of factors that affect identity and morale.

Following on from this, again in this curious mixture of privilege and pressure, I would say that clergy often do not realise, and thereby neither do their congregations, the effect of daily being admitted to the innermost thoughts, worries and concerns of their church members or parishioners. For example, what is the long-term effect on ministers of visiting the bereaved, leading and preaching at countless funerals and engaging in pastoral follow-up? There is a right sense in which clergy get used to this, though still making careful preparation and giving of their best. But it is possible to forget that for the people concerned, whether they are people of much, little or no faith, such an occasion carries deep, fundamental desires, fears, hopes and grief. For them, the occasion is an intense 'one-off' event in life. How is it for the minister?

The gift of liturgy

The role of liturgy may be crucial here. Liturgy and ritual can help clergy cope with and not be overwhelmed by the nature of the occasion. I can think of many demanding experiences from my own ministry: for example the funeral of a four-month-old baby as a result of cot death, the child being the same age as my first-born son. His mother and my wife had attended the same ante-natal class. Then I think of the middle son of one of my churchwardens, who died aged twenty-one in a car crash, in which his younger brother was the driver and suffered only a broken nose. There was the promising young black actor who died of cancer, also aged twenty-one. His funeral was attended by over four hundred young men and women in their twenties, and his mother, herself only thirty-six, wanted a framework of liturgy that would help express both grief and hope, but at that stage had no personal Christian faith herself. In all these situations, the gift of liturgy was an enormous help to me in my role. At an even more personal level when facing the deaths of my own parents aged seventy-two and eighty-six respectively, my desire to speak at their funeral services in appreciation of all they gave me in terms of security of life and an example of faith was helped by the liturgy used, as well as by the personal support I received.

Any minister reading this would add his or her own examples. The point I am making is that liturgy, rightly understood and used, is a wonderful gift and can be an enormous help. Nevertheless, clergy need to acknowledge, more than is often the case, both the pressures as well as the privileges of continuous involvement with people in situations of grief and loss, and the effect on their own faith journey and morale. Something gets inside that has to be processed one way or another, and if that does not happen in a healthy and constructive way it can lead to the depression, exhaustion, breakdown or burnout that John Sandford writes about. In short, in order to sustain an effective and healthy ministry over a period of time, we need to pay a right kind of attention to taking care of ourselves.

As Andrew Clitherow writes: 'Again we are reminded that it is not selfish but essential that the priest should care for him or herself. It is not a distortion but the foundation of our ministry.

For it is the will of God that we should become whole as the Spirit of creative love operates upon us.'[4]

To this matter we now turn in detail in the next chapter.

3
Taking care of ourselves

cknowledging personal need is hard for many people, especially in a world where success and image hold increasing sway. For ministers, what seems to happen sometimes is a redoubling of efforts and a driving of themselves even harder, rather than an admission that ministry or some other aspect of life is tough. The truth is that being a giver or carer can unwittingly become a defence against vulnerability. The empathy and compassion, which ministers often exercise very well in respect of others, is often sadly lacking or a low priority for themselves. Many ministers seem to have great difficulty in giving proper attention to their own needs and feelings.

In exploring why this can be the case, I want to begin by looking at an issue identified in the previous chapter, that of the blurring of boundaries. Why this is a particular issue for ministers may be to do with the way in which the biblical tradition is sometimes understood and interpreted. It is possible after all to cite biblical precedent for not setting limits and boundaries. Did not Jesus in the Sermon on the Mount speak about going 'the extra mile'? (Matthew 5:41–42). In the farewell discourses in St John's gospel, as Jesus gives the disciples a new commandment to love one another, that might mean literally 'laying down our lives for our friends' (John 15:12–17). These and other passages suggest high expectations of ministers and that could include unlimited availability, with time for and attention to self being low on the agenda, if present at all.

However, in the well-known incident, recorded in Luke 10: 38–42, of Jesus visiting Mary and Martha's home, we note Jesus' response to Martha's resentment at Mary's inactivity as she sits at the Lord's feet. 'Martha, Martha, you are worried and distracted by many things; there is need of only one thing' (vv. 41–42). In as many words Jesus is saying: 'Martha – relax, learn to love and take care of yourself; you're pulled apart by too many distractions.' Martha is part of the human predicament of getting caught up in too much caring at the expense of paying proper attention to the need for stillness in the presence of Christ. Jesus can say this to Martha with all integrity because, although his ministry is marked by total self-giving, he embodies also a self-emptying (Philippians 2:5–11). Part of what his incarnation means is that his human space, time and love were limited just as ours are. He had to learn to pace himself as we do. The problem for many ministers is that while this may be understood at a theoretical, even at what might be called a theological level, at a more emotional level apparent inaction or non-availability can lead to guilt for the self, disappointment for others, or disillusionment for ministers, when they do not meet the needs perceived to be there.

Similarly, in Paul's intensely personal second letter to the Corinthians, what is he saying about himself when he says: 'I will most gladly spend and be spent for you'? (2 Corinthians 12:15). In the previous chapter he described some of the pressures and demands of apostolic ministry including working so hard there was no time for sleep (2 Corinthians 11:27). Yet Paul clearly feels hurt and disappointed by the way in which the Christians at Corinth have treated and are still treating him. He too has needs and feels they do not value him or understand the pressures of ministry.

From St Paul again, in the powerful and moving farewell address to the Ephesian elders, there is a clear message: 'Keep watch over yourselves and all the flock of which the Holy Spirit has made you overseers. Be shepherds of the church of God, which he bought with his own blood' (Acts 20:28). Effective pastoral care of others is impossible if ministers are themselves unfit, and are not taking care of all that makes them the people they are and are becoming.

In the fast-paced, stress-filled world in which we find ourselves, there has perhaps never been a more important time to take these matters seriously, for the sake both of the minister, and of those for whom he or she is a role model in Christian living in a frenetic world. Paying a right attention to the inner life of the minister is not only part of the biblical pastoral tradition – similar messages come through from the early centuries of the Christian Church. For example, Gregory the Great (540–604) focused mainly, in his influential *Pastoral Rule*, on the duties and qualities of the bishop as a shepherd of souls. In this leadership task he saw the specific hazard of pastoral ministry as being so exclusively directed to other's needs that one's own health and well-being could be at risk. 'In restoring others to health by healing their wounds, he must not disregard his own health . . . let him not, while lifting up others, fall himself . . . The greatness of certain men's virtues has been an occasion of their perdition, in that they have felt inordinately secure in the assurance of their strength, and they died suddenly because of their negligence.'[1]

These writings for 'secular' (i.e., non-monastic) clergy had an influence almost as wide as Benedict's Rule for monks. Similarly, John Chrysostom (347–407) who in 398 was appointed Patriarch of Constantinople, argued that: 'The priest's wounds require greater help, indeed as much as those of all the people together . . . because of heavy demands and extraordinary expectations associated with the pastoral office.'[2] Coming from far back in our Christian history, this writing is full of practical wisdom about the duties and pitfalls of a pastor. It sets out excellent advice about preaching, as well as detailing the high spiritual standards required of leaders, and the consequent demands and responsibilities as well as joys laid on them. It remains one of the great classic works of pastoral theology.

The message is clear then that care of others and care of self cannot be separated. A right kind of self-love and self-care is vital. As Andrew Irvine puts it in *Between Two Worlds*: 'Self-denial is not the same as self-neglect . . . the world of action must decrease so the world of being can increase.'[3] Too many ministers have, I suspect, confused self-denial and self-neglect, and they and others have suffered as a result.

Few, I imagine, would disagree with the second half of the above quotation but the issue remains: how can this be possible, in the sheer busyness and sometimes seemingly unrelenting nature of church life and ministry today? From my personal experience, as well as observation of others, it seems that ministerial overload often expresses itself in three ways: an over-full schedule of church work; under-scheduling time with spouse and family; or no scheduling at all, when it comes to doing things for personal nourishment. If the outer and inner worlds of doing and being (to use Jungian terminology) have become out of balance, how can healing and restoration of balance take place?

I believe that a fresh look at the life and ministry of Jesus can help us rediscover who we are, how we can look after ourselves and how we can seek to live a more balanced, integrated life in the world, gladly embracing our humanity. Perhaps what many clergy need is permission, and sometimes specific help and guidance, to seek this sense of integration, to nurture their inner world and, in an appropriate way, replicate Jesus' approach to life. As St Paul wrote: 'Let this mind be in you that was also in Christ Jesus' (Philippians 2:5).

The gospels clearly show that Jesus regularly found time to rest and to renew his energies. Looking for example at the first five chapters of St Mark's gospel, Jesus' pattern is of intense ministry followed by significant time set aside for reflection, prayer, fasting and solitude. This pattern is then repeated at regular intervals throughout his ministry. Jesus took care of himself. He would go to a quiet place, to take time to be reminded of who he was and how much he was loved by the Father, as well as to seek the Father's will on specific matters such as the choosing of the twelve apostles (Mark 3:13–19). Having refocused and been freshly energised – even if sometimes those times apart got interrupted! – he could return to the fray with a renewed perspective (Luke 4:42–44). If Jesus needed to invest time regularly in keeping his calling clear, discerning priorities and keeping distractions and temptations at bay, how much more is that important for people in Christian leadership today!

Taking a specific example from these early chapters of St Mark, in his account of the stilling of the storm (Mark 4:35–41) we find Jesus once again taking himself and the disciples away from the crowds whom he has been teaching. A storm arises on the lake, a not infrequent occurrence, and where is Jesus? In the boat, at the stern, asleep! At this moment he is not engaged in ministry to others – not even to the disciples who are crying out for his help. It seems that before calming the storm, he finds a place of calm for himself.

Could it be that there are times in ministry when a conscious decision needs to be taken to be in the 'back of the boat', taking a break from active engagement in ministry even when the needs are staring us in the face? A time for remembering who and whose we are, because it is crucial, given the tendency for ministers to lose their personhood in their work, to remember that God loves us for who we are, not for what we do.

Jesus' ministry, life and style appear to be in stark contrast to the style and approach of many ministers today. Jesus calmed the storm – but only at the appropriate time. Jesus did not hurry into action. Jesus slept until he was needed. The pace of his ministry was characterised by peace, patience and attentiveness. Ministry today seems too often to reflect what is going on in the world at large – driven by speed and restlessness. So changing the pace is an intentional act – it will not happen by accident or drift.

It has been suggested that Jesus' model of taking care of himself contains a four-step process, described by means of the mnemonic 'BREW':

Be still;
Receive the Father's love;
Embrace God's gift of personhood;
Welcome the day and its opportunities to give and receive blessings.

From this rhythm of intense ministry balanced with the need for reflection in one form or another, it seems to me that there are three key dimensions to Jesus' life that helped to sustain him in his ministry. First, in Jesus we see someone totally committed to the priority of doing his Father's will. Second, within that total commitment, he did not neglect his own physical and emotional needs. Third, he developed significant relationships with the twelve apostles and others close to him like Mary, Martha and Lazarus, who provided him with a bolthole at Bethany.

These three dimensions of Jesus' life and ministry might provide a check list, a 'toolkit' that ensures not simply survival but also the means of sustaining an effective ministry, bearing in mind, as Henri Nouwen has written, 'Ministry can be fruitful only if it grows out of a direct and intimate encounter with our Lord.'[4] Or, to quote Lesslie Newbigin: 'The minister's leadership of the congregation in its mission to the world will be first and foremost in the area of his or her own discipleship, in that life of prayer and daily consecration which remains hidden from the world but which is the place where the essential battles are either won or lost.'[5]

Doing the Father's will

Knowing the guilt that can immediately assail clergy as well as other Christians when it comes to reflecting on their own spiritual lives, what clergy need is a spirituality that both sustains, and empowers them for, effective leadership and ministry. A realistic expectation and honest self-knowledge is required, combined with an appropriate 'growing' spirituality.

I believe that the crucial factor in the effectiveness of the local church is the quality of its spirituality, which can be defined as an understanding of how encounter with God takes place and how such an encounter is sustained. Thus what is going on or not going on for its leaders in this area is of enormous significance.

In this transition time for church, society and the role and identity of the clergy, it is important to consider what is realistically available to help spiritual growth and development. Mike

Riddell comments: 'When the heart is captivated by Christ, then all of existence becomes a resource for growing in depth and understanding.'[6] This speaks of a rediscovery of who we are in Christ – a reminder of Jesus' call to the first disciples to be with him as well as go in his name (Mark 3:14). Part of this rediscovery may reveal a need to let go of any distorted view of 'the Father's will' and his expectations of us. As we have already observed, how we understand and 'see' God will affect the way we live.

I believe a number of deliberate steps can be taken to develop a more accurate view of the Father's will and purpose.

A visiting, or revisiting, of the spiritual disciplines

Richard Foster believes that it is the classical disciplines of prayer, meditation, Bible study, simplicity, solitude, submission, service, confession, worship, guidance and celebration that can promote a deep inner life, 'drawing us inward into the transformation we need', and hearing 'the call outward into the ministry we need: healing the sick, suffering with the broken, interceding for the world'.[7]

If this sounds like more pressure, Foster's intention is just the opposite. If the response coming to mind is 'I'd love to engage with these resources but ministry is so pressurised today that I haven't got time', maybe the question that needs to be asked is 'Can we afford not to?' These disciplines are about restoring perspective on life and ministry, allowing God to come close again, taking an opportunity to get off the treadmill and to start to enjoy life again, if that capacity has been lost or sidelined. There will need to be a conscious commitment to making this a priority. It will not happen by chance. Again, to quote Nouwen, 'It is from the transformed or converted self that real ministry flows.'[8]

It may mean honestly asking tough questions, like:

What occurs in my life that nurtures me spiritually?
What occupies the space at the centre of my life?
What drives and motivates me?

Keeping a spiritual journal

One expression of this conscious commitment for me has been in keeping a spiritual journal. My spiritual director encouraged me to do this many years ago but, to be honest, intention won the day over reality for much of that time. However, following my three-month sabbatical in 1999 I began to keep a journal on an almost daily basis.

What is fascinating to me is that the value of such a discipline crops up in the most unexpected places. 'How writing a diary gave me new hope' – so ran the headline in the April 2001 edition of *Good Housekeeping* magazine! The article that followed reflected the way in which the long tradition of diary- and journal-keeping has received fresh impetus from more recent developments in the field of psychoanalysis. The seminal figure is undoubtedly Carl Jung. His encounter with his own unconscious was aided by keeping a journal of his fantasies. This practice was taken up and formalised by the American analyst, Ira Progoff, who is well known for promoting the use of journalling as a vehicle for self-realisation. Another approach to journalling, but also with a Jungian influence, is that of the psychoanalyst Marion Milner. An alternative approach, which places more emphasis on the journal as an aid to personal creativity, has been inspired by the work of Otto Rank.

Recognising that we live in a fast-changing and increasingly stressful and fragmented society, it seems many are finding that to keep a journal can be an important tool for the health of both body and mind. The American Medical Association carried out some research and found that writing down thoughts and feelings about particularly stressful events helped improve the health of people with chronic conditions such as asthma and arthritis. It also boosted the immune system when patients wrote for as little as twenty minutes a day over a period of two weeks.

Within the Christian tradition, both Catholic and Protestant, there are well-known examples of journal-keeping. Some of them, like those of John Wesley, George Whitfield, Søren Kierkegaard and George Fox have become spiritual classics. More recent examples from within the Roman Catholic tradition include Thomas Merton's *The Asian Journal*[9] and Henri Nouwen's *The Genesee Diary*.[10]

What both 'secular' and 'spiritual' seem to have in common when it comes to journalling is that what is written acts like a mirror. Through the journal's pages we may discover more of who we really are. Commenting on this, Henri Nouwen says: 'I have little to say about events, good or bad, creative or destructive, but much about the way I remember them – that is, the way I start giving them form in the story of my life.'[11] The late Bishop John Robinson described his own journal as 'something very different from a diary, which has always oppressed me. There you feel you have got to record something every day, whether there is something worth saying or not.'[12]

For me, keeping a journal is sometimes just a page reflecting on the key moments and encounters, positive and negative, of the previous day. At other times, it will include reflection on my Bible reading or devotional book. I also use the Ignatian recommendation of calling to mind five good things from the previous day, and one instance where I could have acted and responded in a better way. Included too are prayers for others and for whatever might be in the news. I find it to be a helpful part of the process of enabling me to prioritise and organise my life and ministry more effectively. Indeed I find the very act of writing slows down the inner revs, brings me to a place of fresh openness to God and increases my capacity for reflection which, as I am an activist by nature, needs all the help it can get!

As Lawrence Osborn has observed: 'It [a journal] is primarily, though not exclusively about yourself. It cannot be exclusively about self for the simple reason that no-one lives an entirely isolated life. Our relationships with others play an important part in making us who we are.'[13]

Perhaps what distinguishes a 'spiritual' journal from a secular one is the acknowledgement that our relationship with God is the central factor in the discovery of self. That which is written, whether apparently mundane or brimming with significance, is done so before God and in the awareness of the spiritual journey we are on with him and in the company of others.

To keep a journal is a discipline and if we choose to embark on this exercise, we need to find a way that 'goes with the grain' of our characters and personalities. So for some the approach will be descriptive – which corresponds to the 'sensing' personality type in Myers-Briggs terms. Others will find a free-ranging, intuitive style appropriate – corresponding to the 'intuitive' type. The 'thinking' type will probably write in a more reflective way and the 'feeling' type will find that just to write is in itself cathartic. If you are a 'pictorial' person, there may be few words but plenty of images and drawings. As Lawrence Osborn again writes: 'The only rule for a successful journal is that there are no rules. In the journal you are completely free to do your own thing.'[14]

What I have come to discover is that without keeping a journal, or having some other equivalent means of reflection and aid to prayer, spiritual growth becomes indiscernible, except in the broadest terms. A discipline that may appear difficult or an extra demand to start with becomes an invaluable part of life. During tough and challenging periods of life, I have found that, having established the discipline of keeping a journal, to be able to write in this way has been cathartic. To record pain, fears and anxieties, as well as tracing the hand of God at work in difficult situations, has been faith-building, seeing God resolve what at first may have appeared to be intractable problems.

To be practical and to prevent keeping a spiritual journal from becoming burdensome, may I suggest the following guidelines:

> *Start out small* – perhaps ten minutes of writing or drawing to start with. If you're still inspired after that time, keep going!
>
> *Be creative* – express yourself both in ways that 'go with your grain' but also in unexpected ways from time to time.
>
> *Make a list* – identify problems or concerns in your life and then distinguish between the urgent and important, the real and the imagined.

Ask yourself a question – get your thoughts flowing by asking a question like: 'How am I feeling about . . . at this point in my life?'

Fill in the blanks – complete a sentence such as 'The most important thing I have to do today is . . .'; reflect at the end of the day 'The best thing that happened to me today was . . .'

Bible study and prayer

The Anglican Ordinal has the bishop ask those he is about to ordain: 'Will you be diligent in prayer, in reading holy Scripture, and in all studies that will deepen your faith and fit you to uphold the truth of the Gospel against error?'[15] The ordained and others in Christian leadership are accountable – but, in reality, who asks questions or gives support in these areas on any regular basis? It is firstly, I believe, in the clergy's own hands to take responsibility for their own personal spiritual growth by means of Bible study and prayer.

In taking responsibility for ourselves, questions need to be asked such as:

Why, how and how often do I study the Bible?

What prevents fruitful personal Bible study and prayer?

Often, ironically, it is preparation for preaching and teaching that can get in the way of meaningful encounter with God through these means. The requirement to communicate regularly on deep and often personal issues, the seemingly relentless nature of preparation and delivery, can mean that all study and praying is geared towards public ministry rather than inner feeding. Of course, on the principle that 'in giving we receive', learning and growing are taking place, but should there not be, as St Bernard put it, time for 'love of God for both our sake and God's sake'?

For some people, teaching is intrinsically bound up with their own spiritual insights. I am someone who often thinks 'I could use that in three weeks' time' when engaged in my own personal devotions! All the time, there is the desire to communicate to others the insight I have just glimpsed. It has come as a great relief and encouragement to realise that this is one sign of having the 'spiritual gift of teaching' (Ephesians 4:11).

Every working life has its rhythms of demands and energy, and the working lives of those in full-time ministry are no exception. If an effective ministry is to be sustained for the long haul, there is a need to build in seasons of greater opportunity for study, for Bible reading and prayer. This could well involve the discipline of blocking out times in the diary well in advance, and treating that 'appointment with God' in at least as serious a way as other appointments. Dr John Stott in *I Believe in Preaching*[16] recommends an overall rhythm of an hour a day, a day a month and a week a year set aside for personal Bible study and prayer. In my experience the hour a day is the hardest to hold on to, yet for our own sakes and that of the ministry to which we are called, maybe a move can take place from being 'too busy to pray and study' to being 'too prayerful to be busy'. We must prioritise the time apart with God.

Recognising our human needs
Physical needs

In these days of greater awareness of the value of 'healthy living', we are very conscious of the importance of physical needs being met. Ironically, however, again because of the pace of life and its demands, they are often the first to be neglected. According to the World Health Organisation, health is not merely the absence of disease, but a state of physical, mental and social well-being – such as in the Christian tradition might be described as wholeness or *shalom*. It is well documented that there is a strong tendency in many clergy to overwork, get over-intense, maybe overeat or drink too much, neglecting both exercise and relaxation. Perhaps the words of Jesus have been misunderstood and misinterpreted: 'My Father is always at his work to this very day, and I, too, am always working' (John 5:17).

Thus, clergy justify taking little or no time off, and the levels of stress increase. Apart from the fact that our bodies are temples of the Holy Spirit (1 Corinthians 6:19), we have a responsibility to ourselves and those close to us to take care of ourselves physically. Roy Williamson, former Bishop of Bradford and later of Southwark, said on one occasion: 'A physically fit minister is far more likely to cope with the demands of ministry. Sadly this often only becomes a priority when a crisis hits.' He knew this only too well from his own experience following a major heart attack.

Sarah Horsman writes: 'It [exercise] increases the capacity of the heart for coping with the strains of emotional effort . . . There are also more immediate benefits from exercise. The level of adrenaline rises during exercise, but falls to a lower level afterwards, so regular exercise has the effect of an overall lowering of the adrenaline level.'[17]

A clergyman I know, who had experienced a near-fatal heart attack, took an hour's exercise around lunchtime each day and if anyone came to see him then, they either had to wait or walk with him! He had learned the hard way, as have others, to take responsibility for his physical well-being, and that exercise became part of the routine of his daily life. We have to respond appropriately according to our circumstances, general health and age, but books like *Living with Stress*[18] can give realistic pointers towards helping us with physical fitness. Eating healthily and unhurriedly also plays its part in this whole process.

As a practical step, if overall health allows, why not commit yourself to some regular exercise each week – even if it is simply a walk in the countryside or somewhere nearby in your lunch hour. Experience the slower pace of a pedestrian and be open to what is around you. Think again of Jesus' life and ministry – one of the things that struck me when I visited Israel for the first time was the vast distances he and the other disciples walked. We have the so-called blessings of faster modes of transport, but have we lost something of the space he gained through physical exercise between appointments?

Intellectual needs

There is a need for people in ministry to continue to grow and develop intellectually, and I will elaborate on this later. Again, some personal responsibility needs to be taken for ongoing theological reflection so that our bookshelves do not betray when we died theologically. It is also important that we engage with the issues of this changing world. If that sounds like yet another pressure to 'keep up our reading' and it seems we can't afford the time in this way, I want again to ask, for our overall well-being and ministry's sake, can we afford not to?

People who are not committed to this kind of lifelong learning are in danger of functioning on yesterday's thoughts, which is good neither for them nor for those whom they lead and care for and to whom they preach. David Fisher has advised: 'We need to become expert at reading and understanding cultural maps.'[19] Gerard Kelly suggests: 'Twenty-first century leaders will find themselves asking constantly, "What have I learned today . . . this week . . . this year?" '[20]

In practical terms, this might mean having a personal reading week or attending a Clergy Reading Week such as many retreat houses have in their programmes. If not a week, then maybe two three-day sessions a year might be possible. A friend of mine takes a day a month as 'thinking time' – doing so as he walks, or in some other context away from home. For others intellectual stimulus might come by means of joining an evening class at a local university or college – on literature, history, philosophy, sociology or in learning another language. Alternatively, why not think of joining a local film society or club? Other ministers I know subscribe to a magazine covering an area about which they know little but which is significant in today's changing world.

Significant relationships

Given that it is relationships that bring us both the greatest pain and the greatest joy in life, for clergy, whose relationships in their caring role can be very draining, there is clearly a need for relationships that nurture, replenish and support. Far too many clergy, either by deliberate choice or by habit, regularly interact with others at levels that leave a deep sense of personal unfulfilment and dis-ease.

A ministry modelled on that of Jesus will always be relational. Recognising that systems and structures cannot and should not be expected to provide everything, I believe clergy need to take responsibility for developing significant and supportive relationships. Obviously, some personality types will find this harder than others but, whatever our temperament, it is clear that such relationships can be life-enhancing.

Looking again to the 'Jesus model', we see evidence of this in the way he chose to spend special time and share significant moments with Peter, James and John. These included moments of great joy and wonder, such as the Transfiguration (Luke 9:28–36), and moments of great pain and stress, nowhere more clearly demonstrated than in his desire for them to be with him in the Garden of Gethsemane (Matthew 26:36–46). Similarly Jesus had his bolthole at Bethany where, just before the events of what we now call Holy Week, Mary, Martha and Lazarus made their home and their friendship available to him (John 12:1–8).

Especially when it comes to the local church, the clergy often seem to be afraid of making significant relationships. Indeed, if I think of my father's generation (he served in ordained ministry from 1946 to 1974), clergy were positively discouraged from having significant friendships in the local church. This thinking still persists today, even being part of some theological college training. In some denominations it is part of the rationale for a minister not staying for more than say five years in one place.

Of course, there are the dangers of a perceived 'favouritism', and people in the clergy's care must be treated even-handedly. All the same, Jesus was a great risk-taker, and no doubt some both within and beyond the apostolic band will have misunderstood his motives. How did the other nine disciples feel when he kept disappearing with Peter, James and John? The concept of clergy as somehow being 'non-relational beings', in the sense of not having significant relationships in the local Christian community, to me betrays a bad theology. There is of course a right sense of being set apart by virtue of ordination, but as I read the New Testament letters of Paul and John in particular, I see many references to close and significant relationships, not least as evidenced by the greetings contained within them. Furthermore, the risk of having no significant relationships can lead to an increase in the sense of separation, isolation and loneliness, both for clergy and their spouses, damaging to personal development as well as effective ministry.

So, how might this issue be addressed? Why not seek out two or three people in your local church whom you have learned to be trustworthy; ask them to pray for you after each service or meet with you at frequent intervals. Be ready to share your heart with them; not strategy – that belongs in other places – but who and how you are.

Building relationships beyond the church community is also important. Relationships and relaxation outside the church context where there are no responsibilities help provide a different, wider view of life. They can also help to restore perspective and remind us that ministry is about the Kingdom of God, which is far greater than local church life and leadership. Henri Nouwen says: 'I am convinced that priests and ministers, especially those who relate to many anguished people, need a truly safe place for themselves. They need a place where they can share their deep pain and struggles *with people who do not need them* but who can guide them even deeper into the mystery of God's love'[21] (italics mine).

We live in an age of 'delayed responsibility'. Credit card use is at an all-time high; we plan to start dieting and exercising and reviewing our spiritual life 'tomorrow', but we have had these plans for the last year – or more! Jesus said we are to love our neighbours *as ourselves,* and part of that looking after ourselves might mean getting a grip on some of the inner chaos and outward pressures that make up life – for our own sakes and that of our ministries.

Behind all I have written in this chapter is a commitment to do all in our power to ensure the pace of life and ministry is sustainable. It is easy to feel overwhelmed or filled with guilt at the good intentions that have not been realised. In his book *First Things First*[22] Stephen Covey points out there are three places where we can fall down in this process of managing our time so that we are taking appropriate care of ourselves. The first is failing to plan in the first place; the second, making inappropriate plans, and the third, having made plans, not sticking to them. What he is saying here is that how we use our time is not simply about how we get tasks done, but about how we approach life, and its consequent impact on us and on others. So, going back to the subject of taking care of our physical needs, often it seems we give attention only when a crisis occurs. We are driven by the urgent rather than the important. Taking care of ourselves means seeing things the other way round, which might mean discontinuing some activities – those which may have an aura of urgency about them but which in reality are a low priority for us – in order that the truly important can have its rightful place.

It is a sobering thought that doing the work of God can destroy the work of God within us. Of course the pace and sustainability issue is not entirely in the minister's hands – but more of it is than we realise. Bill Hybels, Senior Pastor of the Willow Creek Community Church in Chicago, in an article entitled 'The art of self-leadership',[23] said this: 'For fifteen years I lived over-committed and out of control, and deep down I kept saying, "Why aren't the elders rescuing me? Don't people see I'm dying here?" But it isn't their job. It's my job.' Later in the same article he wrote: 'The best gift you can give the people you lead is a healthy, energised, fully-surrendered, focussed self. And no-one else can do that for you.'

Henri Nouwen again has some wisdom for us: 'We have indeed to fashion our own desert where we can withdraw every day, shake off our compulsions and dwell in the gentle healing presence of our Lord. Without such a desert we will lose our own soul while preaching the gospel to others.'[24] Mary Anne Coate adds: 'In short, we have to love and take care of ourselves. Often it is the acceptance of this principle that is the most difficult first step; after this the "how to do it" becomes relatively obvious.'[25]

In addition to suggestions already made in this chapter, below are some more 'how to do it' ideas that might help make a difference. 'Pic'n'mix' as seems helpful!

- Commit one regular piece of your time – a morning or evening a week – to re-rooting your relationship with God.
- Intentionally slow down at points during the day. Set aside a few moments two or three times a day for brief reflection. Allow space between appointments to reflect and prepare – learn to practise 'sanctified negligence'! Moments of respite will make us more effective in ministry.
- Have on display in your study or office words of encouragement and pictures to help resist the rush of life.
- Learn to say 'no' more often when asked to do something. Because we *can* do something doesn't always mean we *should*. The need is not the same as the call.
- Learn to enjoy and appreciate life. The author Alan Bennett has a telling quote that many people go through life 'not quite enjoying it'.[26] Compare 1 Timothy 6:17: 'God . . . richly provides us with everything for our enjoyment.'
- Commit to a small group where there is both prayer and accountability. Find/create safe places to rejoice and weep, where stories can be shared of hard and joyful aspects of ministry and discipleship, where you can pray and be prayed for, where you can be known and truly loved.
- So much of ministry is visible to someone – so practise secret service and secret giving, hidden acts of kindness.
- Switch off the doorbell, put the answerphone on at meal times, when taking personal time out and when engaging in personal prayer.
- Be proactive in looking at an upcoming period of time – the next week, month, three months – otherwise the diary and calendar can wrongly rule our lives. Put in as priorities days off, holidays, key family commitments (birthdays, anniver-

saries, sports days, concerts etc.). Many problems occur when ministers operate only reactively.

- Draw up a schedule and prioritise for the week, building in 'crisis time' for the unexpected, because somewhere that will happen in the course of a week. Reflect on it and review it. If facing something or a number of things that are difficult and demanding or unpleasant, balance them with things that are positive and life-enhancing.
- Ensure a minimum of one clear day off each week on the Sabbath principle of no work or contact with work unless it is vital or an emergency. In addition, schedule in either two full days off together once a month, or two or three four-day breaks away each year, apart from holidays.
- Book an annual retreat for the inside of a week.
- Every two months have a day put aside to catch up with paperwork – file, act on, throw away papers as appropriate.
- Review every three months or so, preferably with someone else, what has been effective in ministry and what has not, so energies can be put into the appropriate areas – what is essential, what is not, what is getting missed out.

Ten commandments for relieving stress

1. Thou shalt not be perfect or even try.
2. Thou shalt not try to be all things to all people.
3. Thou shalt leave undone things that ought to be done.
4. Thou shalt not spread thyself too thin.
5. Thou shalt learn to say 'no'.
6. Thou shalt schedule time for thyself and thy supportive network.
7. Thou shalt switch off and do nothing regularly.
8. Thou shalt be boring, inelegant, untidy and unattractive at times.
9. Thou shalt not feel guilty.

And especially:

10. Thou shalt not be thine own worst enemy.

4
The nearest and dearest

The occupational hazard of ministry is that ministers are so often better at ministering to others than to themselves and their nearest and dearest.[1]

Those who are familiar with the parochial ministry will know how quickly an imbalance between work, home and recreation can, in a relatively short period of time, render the most enthusiastic and imaginative priest exhausted and disillusioned.[2]

While not in any way wanting to suggest that home and family life is intrinsically more difficult for the minister than for anyone else, nonetheless there are some distinctions that need to be understood. It is important to note that the changes in society and church life already observed are affecting both how clergy and their families are seen and how they see themselves. Wanda Nash rightly makes the observation that there is perhaps less need nowadays than there may once have been to insist that clergy marriages are exactly the same as others: 'It used to be popular for women to say "I am married to a priest for sure, but my marriage is no different from that of my friends whose husbands are teachers or bank managers or postmen or doctors".'[3]

My personal experience, growing up as an only child in a vicarage, then having been in full-time stipendiary ministry in a variety of settings since 1973 and being married with two, now grown-up, sons, is that the positives far outweigh the negatives. It is important, however, to take a realistic look at this area of the minister's life, and again to ask what levels of support and input from outside should be available, as well as what differences the minister and his or her family can make, if there is recognition of a need for change.

For the purposes of this chapter, my focus is the ordained person in full-time stipendiary ministry. I fully recognise and welcome the fact that nowadays there are a variety of expressions of ordained ministry, and I hope that connections can be made with the material here that will be helpful and relevant for others.

Distinctive factors

What then are some of the distinctive factors that can impinge, either positively or negatively, on the personal and family life of the minister?

First of all, the ordained ministry is one of the few professions where the person is potentially available 24 hours a day to the public. A call, whether at the door or on the telephone, may be trivial but equally it could literally be a matter of life or death. It could be from someone within the church community or it may be a total stranger. As the number of full-time clergy in most denominations decreases, the incidence of these calls will increase as part of the overall workload. The situation also reflects the way in which ordained ministry is probably the profession with the fewest 'boundaries'. People are not confined by appointments, and so the perception can be that whenever the minister is at home, whether on duty or not, he or she is available. I well recall an incident early in my time as a vicar: one bank holiday I was doing some much-needed gardening when a parishioner walked round to where I was at the back of the house: 'I hope you don't mind me disturbing you when you're working but I thought I'd find you at home so I popped round to ask you a few questions because I'm not at work today.' Reflecting later on that incident I realised it contained within it all kinds of assumptions about total availability and boundaries, not to mention a certain confusion about work and leisure!

Other Christian families may choose to operate an open-house policy, but that very choice somehow enables them also to shut the door and protect the boundaries more easily. Most clergy are (rightly) committed and devoted people, understanding themselves to be living in response to a call, rather than simply doing a job or developing the best career possible. Clergy want in the best sense to be available, but as a result the silent victims can often be the spouse and children. If it is argued that there are no limits as to what God might require of the minister, on the same basis there are surely no limits to what it means to be a spouse or parent. So, given that 24-hour availability is the expectation, and ministers know this – at least in theory! – when they are going into it, how can this be handled?

A useful starting strategy might be to keep a note of all the calls, at the door and on the phone, over a four-week period. Then look back and see which ones (with hindsight) needed dealing with urgently and which could have been left. On from this, let the church or churches for which you are responsible know that between certain hours they are likely to get an answerphone – whether that be at mealtimes or some other times in the day you wish to protect. Some clergy have a separate line with a phone number that is not known to parishioners or church members but only to family and friends.

Experience seems to show that the outcome of putting boundaries in place is not likely to be catastrophic. It may even mean clergy are more available, in the sense of being fully present, rather than resentful at yet another intrusion into home and family time.

Second, work patterns for the clergy are different from those of most professions. While other professions may involve some weekend work, it is usually on a rota/on call basis, whereas for the clergy and their families it is the norm. Similarly, evenings often seem in short supply for clergy, as they are taken up with meetings or pastoral and evangelistic work which cannot be carried out in the daytime. Moreover, periods like Christmas and Easter are particularly significant and potentially pressurised times, whereas for the majority of the population they offer the possibility of holiday and recreation.

Before commenting on the possible disadvantages arising from this, I believe it is important to say that clergy are in a privileged position in being able to order and determine some at least of their pattern of work, in relation to their home and family life. There is a degree of flexibility not available to many people, so that, for example, if the minister's spouse does not go out to work or does not work full-time, they may be able to share lunch together regularly. In terms of child-care, the minister may be able regularly to pick the children up from school or make a meal more easily than his or her counterpart in some other professions.

Having said that, spouses and children can easily feel resentful that they are victims of a work pattern unlike most other people's, and when communication gets reduced to post-it notes left on the fridge, it signals a major problem. Given that local church ministry is never going to be a 9-to-5 set-up – and that is part of its attraction and stimulus – are there ways of dealing creatively and positively with these conditions?

As with so much else, communication is the key. A good starting point will be the family facing together the fact that, as with many jobs, there will be seasons of busyness, where the family appears to come second. They can agree to make the most of the positives those seasons bring, and plan that those busy times will be compensated for. On a week-to-week basis, looking to ensure that not all evenings are spoken for by church commitments and putting home time in the diary can help. Some ruthless pruning may need to take place. The church community may need to be encouraged to understand that it is a church leader's responsibility to manage their household well and care for their needs as a top priority (1 Timothy 3). As Andrew Irvine puts it, 'As important as the task of ministry is, the responsibility to the family is greater.'[4]

Third, the sense of ministers and their families being public property brings both great opportunities and huge pressures. It is, for example, a great privilege to become a recognised part of a Christian community more easily and quickly than the average lay person joining a new church. Close, intimate involvement in people's lives at both moments of celebration and moments of pain is not something afforded to many people. That ready-made community can also be a source of baby-sitting, help, advice and support in a whole number of ways, particularly if there is openness on the part of the minister and the family.

But there is also the 'goldfish bowl' syndrome, where people can have unrealistic expectations of the minister and his or her family. The reality is that clergy and their families are as human as anybody else – they feel the same hurts, disappointments and heartaches, stresses and strains, and make mistakes like anyone else. At one extreme, some people, perhaps because of problems or disappointments in their own home or family situation, project their expectations of perfection on to the minister's family. They are supposed to be some kind of 'holy' family. That clergy some-times collude with this, and thereby put themselves and their families under even more pressure, does not help. It seems to me that, without an inappropriate wearing of our hearts on our sleeves, there could be more self-disclosure that says 'We really are human like the rest of you.'

The climate does seem to be changing for the better, with minister, spouse and family able to be more themselves than was once the case. But still one hears stories of insensitive parishioners criticising a spouse for what they wear in church, for the fact that they go out to work or do not in some way fulfil the particular expectations of some church members. Church members may also feel able to give advice to the minister's children, about matters such as their behaviour, appearance or style of clothing, and may be quick to make sure their parents know if there is something to report!

Overall, we have been very fortunate in where we have lived, but I do remember one occasion when one of our sons, in his early years at school, committed some minor misdemeanour. The response of his teacher was: 'I wouldn't have expected that of you, since you're a vicar's son.'

Other church members who are also parents may feel a sense of relief when the minister's child displays some rebelliousness! It is a very public life we are talking about, with privileges and pressures, and communication within the family about aspects that are unreasonable or potentially unbearable is important. We may not be able to stop others peering into the goldfish bowl, but we can and should protect the privacy of our families, especially that of our children.

The public and private can also get mixed up as a result of the minister often working from home. Home for most people is a refuge from the work environment, though in recent years, as a result of our expanding contract culture, more and more people are also doing their paid work there. Interestingly, a recent study has found that despite the initial attraction of not having to go out to work, with the promise of more freedom and less stress, many outworkers are working longer hours than their office-based counterparts. This will come as no surprise to many clergy and their families, for whom this has long been their experience.

For the clergy, where they live can represent parish office, confessional, counselling place and study as well as home. More recently designed clergy houses have the office/study near the front door and separated off from the rest of the house. However, in other cases, the minister's working space is just another room, sometimes even upstairs, and people may not only have to come through a hallway but maybe even pass through other family areas to get there. This has the potential for intimate details of family life to be exposed to public scrutiny in a way that is not the case for other families. Positively, working from home can speak about the interrelatedness of all our actions, but it can also become intrusive and for the spouse and children cause not a little resentment.

From personal experience and observation of others, it seems to me that this blurs boundaries in another way too. Problems that belong in the study spill over into the kitchen, the living room and even into the bedroom. If the minister is out or not available, there are often expectations that the spouse or children will provide information, answer questions, take messages or provide a listening ear to a troubled parishioner. What action we take in response to this scenario will vary according to circumstances and location.

Having worked from home for the first 19 years of ordained ministry, I am now a firm advocate wherever possible of having an office that provides some kind of base in the church itself. It may take time for a local church community to accept this and to see its benefits and for us as ministers to learn to work differently, but the benefits far outweigh the costs. The whole issue of boundaries gets more clarity, efficiency is increased, and both for the minister and family home can be more like home should be, with the study becoming a place for reflection, preparation, reading and prayer – in short a sacred space. Where such a development is not possible, doing all we can to preserve appropriate privacy should be a high priority, along with clear communication for the spouse and family. One minister I know found things improved enormously when he simply made clear that when his study door was open, he was interruptible and when it was closed, he was not, except in an emergency.

Sources of support

If these are some of the distinctive features of the lives of clergy and their families, what are the consequences and implications? For me, particularly given the public nature of their lives, it is important to look at where the spouse and family find support and input for themselves. A survey from Australia back in the mid 1980s, quoted by Robin Pryor, revealed that 57 per cent of ministers indicated that their spouse was the 'most important source of support and encouragement'.[5]

I would not be surprised if a similar response was the case in England today, but it begs the question, 'That's all very well, but from where do spouses get *their* support?' A spouse can feel that, unlike everyone else in the church, they do not have a minister to turn to. Ministers can get so involved in others' lives that the spouse's perception is that others matter more and have first claim on the minister's time and energy. What is more, the children can feel that they share a parent with many other people and as a result can feel marginalised, even unloved. What does it mean emotionally to have a 'representative of God' as husband, wife or parent? There are often complexities at a deep level, understanding what it means to relate to someone in a family set-up one moment and at the altar or in the pulpit at the next. This can be particularly hard when someone comes into ordained ministry in midlife, having pursued another career. As one person said to me, with some feeling, 'I didn't marry a minister, I didn't even marry a practising Christian and now look what's happened!'

There is so much that is good and healthy in clergy families, but it seems to me that support and input is needed from a number of sources, and at various levels, according to people's personality and circumstances. The first thing to recognise is that a minister cannot and should not be pastor to their own family, just as a doctor is not allowed to treat family members, nor a psychiatrist to act as therapist to relatives. As Andrew Irvine puts it:

> The loss of objectivity and the need for all parties involved to have open freedom of expression without fear of repercussions within the home make this especially true for the clergy. The clergy family must have the opportunity to seek pastoral care and advice from a source that they perceive to be objective and without bias ... It is important that those of the minister's household be encouraged to find their pastoral caregiver in someone other than their partner or parent. Opportunity to seek objective guidance at this level may well prevent crisis at another.[6]

Often it seems a general support is offered by the denomination of which the minister is a part, but this can be so vague and imprecise that it is of no real value. This might include an occasional clergy wives' gathering, often held at a time when the majority cannot attend, and which by being so named also excludes the husbands of people in ordained ministry. Or there's a 'We're here if you need us' kind of approach, which is well meant, but can send out signals that it is only for emergencies, and that it might anyway be perceived as a sign of weakness to ask for help.

In the light of this, it is not unreasonable to expect that a counselling service should be made available for clergy and their families, and I will refer to some models for this in the next chapter.

One further source of support, which has been much appreciated in recent years, is the Society of Martha and Mary. This is a charity based in Devon that offers support, counselling and residential facilities for clergy and their families. 'We exist because ministry is a demanding vocation, very fulfilling but at times draining and isolated,' says the Society's publicity. With this in mind, they offer regular '12,000 mile services' and a range of other pastoral programmes.[7]

I will also discuss later the need for clergy fraternals and chapters to change their ethos to provide a more open and supportive context for clergy. Something similar could be encouraged among those spouses who would value it – to pray, share, enjoy one another's company and, as appropriate, moan together! There is evidence of a growing numbers of 'cells' where either three or four clergy couples meet. These too are opportunities to share, pray and offer support to one another.

One northern diocese offers to all clergy and their spouses the possibility of a 'pastoral companion'. These are trained people, lay and ordained, whose names are contained in a booklet available to all clergy, and normally all contact is entirely confidential.

Along with the right expectation that there should be care from within the structures, there are also ways in which the minister and family members can take initiatives. As one example of this, I quote from personal experience. For six years between 1986 and 1992, during the time when I was Officer for

Evangelism in Carlisle Diocese and Vicar of a small rural parish, our family lived in an extended household community with another family. One of the things we put in place early on was to have a clergyman and his wife, who had themselves had experience of community living, as mentors to our household. They would come about three times a year, spend time with us all together, and as we wished, time with each person separately. That objective care and support was invaluable and I wonder whether something similar could not be encouraged and modelled as a viable means of support and care for clergy and their families.

Replenishing relationships

It is not only for the clergy that relationships can be draining, but for their families as well. This arises out of the inevitable overlap there is between work, home, social and church life. Family members too need opportunities for relationships that replenish. The minister may not be able to be the pastor to his or her own family, but they have as much right to expect support from within the congregation as anyone else. Here there is, it seems to me, another fundamental ecclesiological issue. Are the clergy family a part of the community, or apart from it? How they perceive themselves, and how they are perceived, might well determine the response of a congregation. The signals that are sent out will be important here.

In the best scenario, individuals within the local church and indeed the church community as a whole can be a great source of support to the spouse and family. A significant recent experience from our own family life bears this out. In December 2000 our elder son Martin, who was then twenty-two, was diagnosed as having chronic renal failure. This came completely out of the blue, as a total shock to us, the prognosis being he would need either dialysis or a kidney transplant in the following six months. Those next six months involved a great deal of anxiety and uncertainty for us all, including our younger son Tim, with both my wife and me being tested for our suitability to be donors.

Subsequently Martin received a kidney donated by my wife, and after various initial setbacks, at the time of writing he is doing well and living a normal life. Our testimony is that, in addition to prayerful and practical support from friends around the world, no family could have been better supported by a church community than we were by that of St Peter's, Shipley – this not simply in terms of prayer but through financial generosity and practical care. But – and this is the important point – many people said how much it had meant to them that we had shared our situation with them. People spoke of having been the recipients of our care and concern over our nine years in the parish, and were delighted to be able to reciprocate. This is something of what it meant to be part of the community, rather than being 'apart from'. Of course, this may not be a model all sit comfortably with, but I believe it has significant New Testament precedent. For instance, in 2 Corinthians, Paul opens his heart and is very vulnerable with the church in Corinth.

However they are found and expressed, safe places for replenishing relationships are vital for our health and well-being. Personal growth can take place in such a context, as time is spent with people who love us for who we are, but who will also be truthful and challenging where and when appropriate. All this is about developing a capacity for relatedness and becoming more fully human.

The minister's part

The most important gift the 'nearest and dearest' can receive, however, is from the minister themselves, and here we come to an area both easily neglected by the minister and carrying with it a strong sense of guilt. This has been hinted at already, but the truth is the family has more right to the love, time and emotional energy of the minister than anyone else. The tragedy is that often all they get are the leftovers. They can then come to feel they are just another part of the problems the minister is dealing with. It is very easy for the level of relationship to lose any sense of intimacy and warmth and become purely functional.

Part of the answer is very simply (simple to say, if not to do!) to ensure proper time off and away from work, time in which the minister is truly present with the family. That is why parts of a day and time snatched here and there are insufficient. Without proper designated time off, difficult pastoral situations remain in the forefront of the mind, and time with spouse or family, like holidays too, can end up being stressful rather than re-creational. As John Sandford[8] puts it: 'It takes longer than that (a few hours) for the invisible threads that connect us to our work to be relaxed, so that new thoughts, new moods, new experiences can find their way in.' He goes on: 'Ministering people are notoriously poor about keeping even one day of the week saved for themselves and their families. They always have a score of reasons why it cannot be done. This or that simply *must* be done.'

Some may have to face the fact that what stops them from addressing this problem is not only that they lose a sense of personal worth when they are not working, and don't like spending time with themselves, but also that they may be using the demands of their work in an attempt to avoid home and family life. A vicious circle can develop here. If the spouse or children already feel neglected or marginalised, that very sense of resentment may increase the possibility of the minister not making more time for them, because it might mean some confrontation and more facing of painful issues. If there is an 'urgent' hospital visit to be done, or a church meeting that 'needs' the minister to be there, with a 'good conscience' an unpleasant confrontation can be avoided. This is nothing other than an escape mechanism, but can come dressed up as 'doing God's work' – which of course supersedes all other responsibilities.

To face and deal with this kind of thing is not easy, and help may be needed as a minister takes a good look to see what inadequacies or personal needs may be being covered up by such total immersion in work. If such things are not faced, a price will be paid later, one way or another – in cynicism, burnout, breakdown or broken relationships. It is trite but true that prevention is better than cure, and the increasing number of marital breakdowns among ministers makes this an urgent issue to be addressed. Being in some sense public property can add extra strain where there are already stresses and difficulties in evidence, with the expectation that somehow things shouldn't go wrong for this so-called 'holy' family.

Although there is much disappointment and hurt when things do go wrong for ministers and their families, in reality very little importance has been attached to providing opportunities for couples to get help, for instance by attending a marriage enrichment course, before things get to breaking point. Many clergy, facing either the descent into a purely functional relationship or worse when things have gone beyond repair, with hindsight blame their over-involvement in ministry work for their failure to realise how unhappy their spouses were. It is all too easy to take for granted our nearest and dearest, especially when life has been busy and we are tired.

Positively, as we have already noted, it requires us to put time with spouse and family into the day as a priority, to compensate for the busy seasons with time out elsewhere, to ensure holidays are sacred, to show our friends who can be part of the replenishing relationships that they are worth more than a quick drink in the pub on a Friday night every third month. It is about keeping free time on birthdays and anniversaries, about writing in the dates of children's sports days and concerts, about regular meals out or visits to the cinema or theatre with your spouse. As children grow older their needs change and how we are available to them has to change with it. What happens is we become less in control! My experience and observation tells me that it is often inconvenient in our terms when our children want or need us. But needed we still are, and available we must be. For teenagers, establishing an identity and place in life can be hard anyway, and being a minister's child can add to those pressures. Never more than at that age and stage do they need to have space to be themselves, and not have to live up to the expectations of peers, church members or parents. Parents, I believe, may need at this point to work hard to protect them from expectations of conformity from others or from themselves.

In the light of this, there are perhaps five gifts a minister can give to his or her children. First, to pray for them each day – that God will give them the capacity not just to survive, but to have the strength and patience to flourish in what can sometimes be a tough environment, and that they will come to follow Christ for themselves, and not simply conform to any expectations or demands imposed by the church. Second, to allow the freedom and space to 'fail'. What drives many minister's children to rebellion and rejection of the church, Christian faith, and even sadly sometimes the family, is the burden of expectation. As I have already illustrated, ministers' children will make mistakes, and a minister who is a parent needs to care more about his or her children than outward appearances, and possible consequent attitudes to his or her ministry. Third, the minister should step in and defend their children when church members overstep the bounds, whether in terms of advice or reprimand. Fourth, and especially as the children get older, the minister should encourage them to build relationships with other adults in the church who can be role models for them. It is also important to ensure they receive input via children's or youth work, where their parents are not involved. This may mean through another church or youth group in the locality. Finally – and it is perhaps a strange-sounding gift – there is the gift of apologising. When the minister gets it wrong, in whatever way, to say, 'I'm sorry. Let's start again' or 'I'm sorry there hasn't been much time recently' can be sufficient to heal what could otherwise fester.

Where faith is not shared

It seems important to acknowledge that while for many spouses, even the majority, a shared Christian faith lies at the heart of the marriage, there is no reason why this should be assumed. It may be that the one called to ordained ministry was not a Christian at the time of marriage and their partner has not subsequently begun any journey of faith. Furthermore, a significant number of clergy spouses I know have found their faith to be challenged or even undermined in the course of their partner's ministry. For some, this is largely a theological or spiritual issue, but for

others it is the Church as an institution, and how it can sometimes treat the clergy and their families, that is the problem. The
public face of the clergy spouse can make it difficult for such
things to be acknowledged, particularly if there is still an expectation that the spouse should go to church, and be involved there
as a result of being married to the minister. A great deal of
sensitivity is required by both partners in order to deal constructively with this kind of situation. Furthermore, it is crucial that
there is better understanding on the part of the local church
community and the wider church, so that undue expectations
and pressures are not put on either partner. One couple I spoke
to had dealt with this issue by making clear, in advance, to the
lay leaders of the church, that the spouse would not be involved
in the worshipping life of the community. Because they made
their position clear, it meant that there was no clash of expectations. The level of understanding and acceptance that was
shown was further underlined by the way in which the spouse
was included in social events and other expressions of
hospitality.

Women ministers and their husbands

Although some denominations have had women as part of their
ordained ministry for many years, from my research and conversations with such ministers it still seems that, both as they enter
ministry and subsequently, difficulties can be encountered that
men do not experience. This often seems to be in relation to
home and family matters. Irvine comments:

> Studies have shown that married working women, with or
> without family, tend to have a higher overall workload than
> their male counterparts. Much of this is due to the expec-
> tation that women are still the primary nurturers in the
> home. The end of the day in the workplace may become
> the beginning of role as wife and mother. Although many
> modern males share more of the domestic responsibility

than past generations, much of the burden still falls to the woman.[9]

Some women ministers experience this expectation acutely, not only within themselves but also because of traditional expectations on the part of the church. Older people particularly may hold on to 'traditional' values and expectations, fuelled by the socialisation of past generations. This is not always intentional, but is so deep-rooted it may take years to change. All this means that there is additional stress for women in ministry because of their gender, and the Church needs to take this more seriously.

When it comes to expectations of the husbands of ministers, it seems these are less than for clergy wives. In the Church of England, this scenario is a comparatively new phenomenon, dating from the ordination of women to the diaconate in 1987 and to the priesthood in 1994. However, what research has been done, coupled with anecdotal evidence, seems to suggest much less in terms of any defined role on the part of the husband, as Sarah Meyrick's somewhat tongue-in-cheek remark suggests: 'The baggage (flower arranging, Mothers' Union, sensible shoes) just doesn't seem to travel across the gender gap.'[10]

Earlier in her book, Meyrick comments: 'The fact that the number of clergy husbands (of whom nothing or little is expected, it appears) has increased, is a huge relief, and the deathblow to old ingrained attitudes.'[11]

With no particular role models in evidence, it seems each husband is on the whole free to create his own role and level of involvement. For some men that freedom is fine, but there are those who do have an identity problem, and there is not a lot of evidence that this is being seriously addressed. In one Anglican diocese, the assistant bishop organised occasional meetings for 'clergy husbands', which were much appreciated as opportunities to talk and share some of the distinctive factors in this situation. However, in another region, one clergy husband's response was: 'I'm not aware of where I can go for support or professional help if I needed it. You have to fend for yourself.' Clearly more work needs to be done as to what parishes make of clergy husbands, and equally what dioceses or their equivalent make of them, so that understanding and support can increase.

Single issues

How does all this relate – if at all – to those who are in ministry but who do not have a spouse or family? Far more clergy are single than is often realised: for example, in one Anglican diocese, of the 22 ordained in 2002, nine were single. This may actually be a reflection of a growing trend in today's world, where more people are single and living alone. It is also important to note that clergy are single for a variety of reasons: some are widowers or widows, others divorced or separated. Some of those who are single may want to marry; others are single by conviction and choice. While it is beyond the scope of this book to go into detail on the issue, there are also a significant number of gay clergy serving in the Church.

Attitudes of parishioners and church members to single clergy seem to vary, depending at least in part on what I have written above. Some single clergy have certainly been made to feel that they are 'second choice', as the parish would have preferred a married person with 2.4 children. However, there are other parishes that positively welcome a single minister and treat them no differently because of their status.

Obviously, single clergy need support in the same way as those who are married. In addition to a spiritual director, a work consultant or support group, the place of friends is crucially important. As I have written earlier, there was, and sometimes still is, the school of thought holding that single clergy, like those who are married, should not have friends in the congregation. I would strongly disagree with this, though again there needs to be professional discretion and the application of common sense. Along with whatever is appropriate locally, single clergy tell me how important it is to work at maintaining friendships from theological college, or the church they were part of before that. To this end, some colleges encourage their graduates to continue meeting in cell-groups twice a year.

One of the greatest dilemmas for single clergy seems to be in the area of time off. A single clergy friend put it this way: 'It is essential that single clergy are disciplined about work, leisure, days off and holidays. I try not to take work into the sitting room but confine it to the study. Also it is easy to allow days off to be taken up with shopping and cleaning. I find that it is money well spent to employ a cleaner, and otherwise try to make time each day for domestic chores.' With no wife or husband present to remind the minister to stop, it seems to be even more important for the single minister to be clear about boundaries, and to put in appropriate safeguards. The assumption that the minister should be totally available if there is no spouse or family to 'distract' or make demands needs challenging, if such an attitude is in evidence in the local church. A linked issue for some single clergy is that it can sometimes feel better to keep working than to do nothing or see nobody during time off.

Although there is a loneliness inherent in ministry, whether for a married or a single person, there are some aspects which the single minister needs to be aware of, and which need to be communicated to and understood by the church, locally and nationally.

In the last part of this chapter, I want to move from the personal to the practical, as it impinges on ministers and their families, namely in terms of housing, finance and the emotions triggered by moving house and location.

Housing

In addition to the public–private issue already explored, there seem to be two practical issues of concern for clergy and their families.

The first is to do with the attitude of the provider of the tied house in which most ministers and their families live. This may be a diocese, a denomination, the local church, or trustees of some kind. In the past, it has sometimes seemed to be the case that the ministers and their families have been expected to make do with standards of repair, heating, plumbing and decoration that church members would not accept in their own houses. This was seen as part of the sacrifice and self-denial expected of the clergy. Nowadays there is increasing evidence of greater thoughtfulness and strategic thinking and planning on the part of the authorities that own clergy housing. It may well be that the house is of a kind that the minister would not have been able to afford, even on a higher salary. That has its advantages, but can also bring its problems. Depending on the area where it is situated, the nature of the house might unhelpfully set the minister and his or her family apart, or conversely they may not be able to keep up with the much better-off neighbours around. There are still plenty of clergy in older houses, who cannot afford to heat them adequately. For single clergy it can be particularly inappropriate to live in a large, cold house. What needs to be remembered is that the minister has not chosen that house, which may be either very suitable or entirely inappropriate; but in the short term, given the salary/stipend that most clergy receive, it is a bonus to have a mortgage/rent-free house provided.

A recent survey has revealed that two in five clergy do own their own property. This is often as a result of coming into ordained ministry from another career. Those who come into ordained ministry later in life and who choose to sell their own property can find a hidden cost in adjusting to no longer having responsibility for and control over their housing. Furthermore, the three out of five clergy who do not have their own property can find that, by the time they reach their early to mid sixties, they have to think about house-hunting and probably moving to a new area at a time when their peers are settling to enjoy the fruits of their labours. This can be very stressful, and while some denominations do provide significant financial and practical help at this point, I believe that more use could be made, for example, of other recently retired clergy to help and advise on the emotional aspect of this significant time of change.

Second, and of increasing concern, is the whole issue of safety and security for clergy and their families. Figures from the year 2000 reveal that 462 attacks took place on clergy of different denominations during that year. So great is the fear that, in some places, clergy are being offered lessons in personal safety by a group called National Churchwatch. (This group was set up to advise clergy of all denominations about security issues, recognising that no theological colleges were offering training in self-protection.) Many attacks take place at or near the minister's home. *The Times* of 1 June 2001 reported the death of a priest in West Kensington in this way: 'Mr Paget operated an "open-door" policy at the Vicarage and allowed young people to stay. He was killed between Tuesday night, following a prayer group meeting on HIV and Aids, and Wednesday morning, when his body was found by a parishioner after the priest missed a Eucharist service.'

At the same time a Roman Catholic priest in Lincoln's Inn Fields spoke of his life being threatened and a colleague being punched in the face. Such is the fear of attack his church had hired a security guard to police the doors of his church. 'It is like being a prisoner,' he said. 'I actually live in the parish behind an iron-grilled gate.' It is incidents and concerns such as these that are prompting some Anglican dioceses to think the unthinkable – to allow clergy sometimes to live in their own houses, or to provide a house that is in a safer environment. For some this is to deny the principle of incarnational living among parishioners, and those who are willing to live in a potentially dangerous setting as part of their calling deserve all the support and encouragement it is possible to give. But it seems it is a time for more flexibility. Certainly as I observe my brother-in-law's situation in an estate parish in south Leeds, the fact that he has a mobile phone and a base within the church but does not live in the parish has not adversely affected his ministry there. On the contrary, after an interregnum of three years and twice failing to make an appointment because no one would live in the vicarage, the parish are delighted to have a gifted minister and there is evidence of new life and hope. It is one thing for the minister to be willing to live in a difficult or dangerous environment, but should the family be put under additional strain? A positive and understanding attitude on the part of the church authorities and the local church, with a concern to provide as good and safe an environment as possible, can go a long way towards helping the minister and family feel valued and cared for.

Finance and debt

A Gallup survey from 1986, prepared for the Archbishops' Commission on Urban Priority Areas, revealed that for 27 per cent of the respondents, personal and family financial problems were a major issue or stress factor. It came third in a list of 12 significant current problems facing people in ordained ministry. Furthermore, 11 per cent indicated that they were dependent on additional financial help from other sources, and 9 per cent were dependent on financial help from parents, in-laws or other family members. Evidence suggests that the situation has worsened since then.

The May 2001 report of the Clergy Stipends Review Group, *Generosity and Sacrifice*, based on a return of over 6,000 replies out of 10,000, revealed 59 per cent of clergy saying that they believed the stipend level should be higher than the current average in 2001 of £17,000. The general picture was that it was difficult to make ends meet if there was no other source of income, for example from a spouse, although some single clergy indicated that they felt quite well off financially. Out of 5,100 working spouses, 8 per cent boosted the income by £20,000 or more; 16 per cent by between £10,000 and £20,000; 15 per cent by between £5,000 and £10,000; and 20 per cent by less than £5,000. It is important to note that in the changing climate in which we find ourselves, some spouses work out of sheer economic necessity while others positively choose to pursue and develop a career. They see this as the outworking of their Christian vocation, which in turn brings a greater sense of identity and often a more objective perspective on parish or local church life. But the financial situation of the minister can in turn lead to resentment on the part of a spouse that the minister is working long hours for small returns or even the resentful feeling that the spouse is subsidising what is properly the church's responsibility. In 2000, 14 years on from the Gallup Report, some 30 per cent of all clergy had received help from charities, family, diocesan funds or parishioners in the previous year; 11 per cent spoke of struggling and being often in debt, and only 13 per cent of those surveyed felt the stipend was adequate, with that dropping to 3 per cent from those ministers who had children. Some bishops say the most regular problem clergy bring them is that of finance or debt, and equivalent senior staff in other denominations would say the same.

It needs to be noted that more than 50 per cent said the level of pay had a bearing on morale; on the other hand clergy are very aware of the tension between the low level of pay and what the church can afford in the current climate. They do not want to be seen as greedy by parishioners, or as a reason for the parish shares and quotas or other contributions to central funds to rise. More recent headlines still, in the autumn of 2001, have talked in terms of £21,000 being a realistic figure for a stipend, that being the current average annual wage in England. Certainly if an adequate stipend were to be paid, the numbers of stipendiary clergy might fall even below the projected reduction, accounting for maybe 1,500 posts over the next 20 years.

Some might want to ask whether these financial problems are the results of poor personal financial management, or evidence of clergy being less resilient now or more unwilling to make sacrifices. Interestingly, since the Second World War, clergy stipends have in fact declined in relation to most other people's income. In 1948 the then Archbishop of Canterbury was concerned that the average clergy stipend was £475, a lot more than the average manual worker's wage of £348.[12] In today's terms that would mean the equivalent of receiving 35 per cent more than the £21,000 figure! It must be stated that one of the improvements in recent years has been better pension provision. This has enabled clergy to retire at 65, rather than have to continue in office indefinitely. However, this has in turn put more strain on central funds as, for example, in the Church of England there are almost as many retired as serving clergy.

Few, if any, clergy go into ordained ministry for its financial rewards and I am aware that what I have written may make rather depressing reading. What is intended is an acknowledgement of some of the problems that some clergy families face as a result of financial pressures that they are sometimes unwilling or even ashamed to admit. I raise this in order that the morale issue can be better addressed and understood both at local and national level. It is not simply a matter of more adequate remuneration, though again there is New Testament teaching that makes clear 'the labourer is worthy of his hire'. It is rather an appeal for sensitive and appropriate support to be given, as people work all this out. If such values are not present it can be another factor that can put further strain on a sometimes already fragile situation.

To move, or not to move: that is the question

It is a well-known fact that moving job and home are two of life's more stressful events and for the minister they usually belong together. Yes, there is the excitement and challenge of a new opportunity for the minister and that is a privilege, but often again it is the spouse and children who can be more affected than is often realised. Because it is expected that most clergy will move a number of times during their ministry, it is often taken for granted as a normal part of life. To acknowledge the loss, sense of uncertainty, and effect of change that people often feel will not change anything external (that is, the call to move) but it can reduce some of the inner strain and bring it into the open.

As a child of the vicarage I moved seven times between birth and the age of twenty, and went to eight different schools. In one way it was exciting to see the removal van again, but in another the long-term effect of lost relationships, having to start again with new ones, and wondering where home really was, left quite a sense of insecurity. One of the remedies – apart from not moving so often! – which we as a family have tried to put in place has been to talk to the children about any potential moves, when they were old enough to understand, and second to seek to avoid disrupting their education as far as GCSE and A-level or other public examinations were concerned. By and large children like the familiar and will always want to stay put, but good communication and consultation can help the necessary adjustments any move brings. Whether we are thinking of the children or the spouse in relation to their careers and personal friendships, it is important to acknowledge the disruption to family life a move can bring and to be aware of what people may be having to give up.

As Sarah Meyrick points out: 'The institutional Church has not always been very considerate about spouses' work when suggesting job moves for the clergy.'[13] Hopefully this situation is improving, and some couples where both have a career make a conscious decision to take it in turns as far as whose job dictates the next move. It is never easy to discern the right moment to move, in relation both to the present appointment itself and personal circumstances. Sometimes the age of the children or the frailty and location of elderly parents can either create windows of opportunity or seem to prevent a move. The age of clergy and their 'marketability' is another factor. Many clergy see the mid-fifties as being the last opportunity to move on, otherwise they are likely to stay put until retirement. Some feel the clerical 'sell-by date' for certain posts is fifty, or even forty-five for some posts of significant responsibility.

The consultancy and support process on moving seems to be fairly haphazard, but it is good to hear of one diocese where, along with the formal tasks regarding the vacancy, the arch-deacon arranges a personal interview with the minister and spouse if they so wish. He comments: 'Clergy need to leave feeling they have been thanked and appreciated.' Again, we see the importance of clergy feeling valued and affirmed. Similarly, more information than is sometimes given about the nature of the new post would help the process of moving into the new situation.

The sheer practicalities of a move can obscure, for the minister and family, emotions that only surface later. Sorting out the files, throwing things away and packing actually open up a treasury of shared experiences with a congregation. This is why a three-month period at least is needed between announcing the departure and actually going, so that period can be a very positive experience for the minister and family, as well as the church. One clergyman described it like this: 'There was a sense of celebrating our time together and being thankful, rather like the best aspects of a funeral service!' Where there have been good and open relationships, it is about understanding the grief that comes from leaving behind significant personal involvement with people, having become part of people's lives, as well as factors like the sheer familiarity with the area.

Having gone through that process and had the necessary farewells, then the word is 'go!' In terms of the gap between leaving one job and starting a new job, having myself made the mistake of too short a gap, I would advise at least three to four weeks, in order to be emotionally and physically ready to start again. It also helps to have given time to and for the family to support them with their adjustments. Some clergy even have a 'mini-sabbatical' at such points, which is another way of managing the change. This is fine as long as it is not at the expense of being with the family at a potentially vulnerable time for them.

The scenarios I have described assume that what is being left behind is being left with some sense of sadness and loss of what has been good. If the period and place of ministry has been less than a happy one, or has perhaps been downright difficult, it will be even more important to work that through with some appropriate help. This is important not only for the minister and the family but also for the place to which they are going, so that unnecessary baggage is not taken and, worse still, put on to the new situation. The minister needs to be 'fit to lead' in a healthy way again.

5

Who cares
for the carers?

n his fascinating account of the vision for and establishment of The London Lighthouse,[1] a hospice and centre for Aids patients, Christopher Spence, its first Director, writes about key values for the staff, paid and voluntary. These include a right to good training, a right to personal development and a right to personal support.

Christopher is now Chief Executive of The National Council for Volunteering, and in conversation with him about both organisations, it became clear how much the Church can and needs to learn from the values evident in both. Christopher spoke of the way in which people think and act best when they feel valued and of how we continually need new experience to face changing situations. Because much of the work of clergy takes us to the edges of life, there is a need here too for pastoral and emotional support. Sadly the Church, which should be in the forefront of modelling such values, is often way behind. A letter to the *Church Times* in February 2002 bears this out: 'In my modest 20 years as a non-stipendiary priest, my stipendiary colleagues have envied me access to the regular words of support that are part and parcel of well-managed secular organisations.'

Establishing a thinking environment

Nancy Kline's work on establishing a 'thinking environment' is a particular resource which embraces the kinds of values of which Christopher Spence speaks. I believe that putting into practice some of her insights could literally be life-changing.

Nancy Kline is a management consultant and the phrase 'a thinking environment' comes from work that she has developed over a 15–year period and has described in her book *Time to Think*.[2] Her basic thesis, which sounds deceptively simple, is as follows:

> Everything we do depends for its quality on the thinking we do first. Our thinking depends on the quality of our *attention* for each other.

A thinking environment is a set of ten conditions under which human beings can *think for themselves* – with rigour, imagination, courage and grace.[3]

The ten conditions are as follows:

1. Attention	– listening with respect, interest and fascination
2. Incisive Questions	– removing assumptions that limit ideas
3. Equality	– treating each other as thinking peers – giving equal turns and attention – keeping agreements and boundaries
4. Appreciation	– practising a five to one ratio of appreciation tocriticism
5. Ease	– offering freedom from rush or urgency
6. Encouragement	– moving beyond competition
7. Feelings	– allowing sufficient emotional release to restore thinking
8. Information	– providing a full and accurate picture of reality
9. Place	– creating a physical environment that says to people: 'you matter'
10. Diversity	– adding quality because of the differences between us

Kline's book describes how these principles can be related to every area of life and work including teams, meetings, supervision, peer mentoring, leadership, family.

Look at the ten conditions again and ask yourself 'Wouldn't it be wonderful for once to be listened to without interruption?' 'Wouldn't it be great to be part of an organisation that offered more appreciation than criticism?' 'Wouldn't it be wonderful to know that those responsible for me and my family's welfare care about the house I live in?' I believe if those in ministry were on the receiving end of such support, it could transform their lives and enable them in turn to offer better support to those in their care.

Reading Kline's book not only made me question how I myself treat and handle others, but also made me wonder if these qualities should be what the structures of the Church should provide for its clergy. This would necessitate appropriate training for bishops, archdeacons, continuing ministerial education (CME) officers and others in line-management roles in their denominations – but if these conditions were modelled by them, what a difference it could make to the morale of clergy and therefore to their parishioners and congregations!

To quote Kline again: 'Such a thinking environment is natural but rare. It has been squeezed out of our lives and organisations by inferior ways of treating each other. Organisations, families and relationships can become thinking environments again, where good ideas abound, actions follow and *people flourish*'[4] (emphasis mine).

In order for this to be the case, we need to be clear on some of the ingredients necessary to turn what sounds wonderful in theory, into reality. To stay with Spence's three 'rights', in the next chapter I will look at issues of ongoing ministerial development and training. Meanwhile in the rest of this chapter I want to explore the area of personal support: what the minister can rightly expect to be available and accessible.

Inter-personal support

Clergy are notoriously independent-minded creatures and, while at one level that may be a help in what can be a lonely task, I believe much more could be made of, and gained from, the support of both peers in ministry and people in other caring professions.

Most denominations have some kind of formal opportunity for such support. In the Anglican Church, dioceses are divided into deaneries and all the clergy are part of a chapter that meets under the leadership of the rural/area dean on a regular basis. In these days of ecumenical partnership, many clergy also meet with the clergy of other denominations working in the same geographical area.

My experience – and I do not think I'm alone – is that the effectiveness of these gatherings varies greatly. Clergy meetings can be tedious, dominated by discussions on funeral fees or the Church's financial problems, and sometimes marked by conflict and a competitive spirit. The end result is that people vote with their feet, because the climate is such that there is little or no possibility of mutual support. This is not perceived as a safe place beyond the local church to share the difficulties and problems as well as the joys and encouragements of ministry. It is tragic that what could be a significant means of support, professionally, socially and spiritually is so often just the opposite. A re-evaluation of the purpose and workings of such gatherings is essential if interpersonal support is to be a reality.

To this end, Steven Croft in his book *Ministry in Three Dimensions*[5] makes a number of practical suggestions that could transform this dimension of support. He says that, first and foremost, *time* must be given to develop relationships and a sense of community. For me, one of my richest experiences of deanery chapter support came through the addition to our normal monthly programme of an annual residential time away. Thirty-six hours, which was a mix of worship, sharing, input and relaxation, made a lasting difference to relationships and mutual support.

Croft goes on to say that *study together* around common themes can be renewing and stimulating. He suggests that about half the time at each meeting should be allocated to this kind of sharing together and study. The business of the meeting should be kept for the other half of the meeting.

The third element is *disclosure* – the willingness to move beyond superficiality, so that personal needs, hopes and fears can be disclosed. Such a trusting climate would mean people could tell their stories, the joys and disappointments they are experiencing. Flowing from that, time to celebrate together, to eat together, to meet socially with spouses could be very enriching.

He suggests too that there must be an element of common *worship*, which is meaningful and connects appropriately with each member of the group. Finally, if the group has formal leadership, time spent by the *leader with each member* outside the meeting will not only enrich the meetings but also give a sense of worth to the individuals concerned. What will emerge from such an approach will be a level of mutual support that could prevent some of the problems of isolation, low morale and stress, which many clergy clearly feel in today's changing world.

Obviously, a particular responsibility rests with the person in charge of such meetings. He or she needs to have a vision for such support and needs to model that in his or her own attitudes, behaviour and approach. But I would also want to say, if that vision does not currently seem to be there, clergy have it in their power to ask for and look for change.

Along with such formal opportunities arising from chapter meetings and fraternals, peer group support can also be possible through people with a particular specialism in ministry or area of work. For example, those working in rural areas, local authority estates, suburbia or the inner city can meet together. In the Diocese of Bradford, a very effective initiative for inner city clergy, started by the former Adviser in Evangelism, Robin Gamble, was entitled 'Behold the Dawn'. This came out of the recognition of some of the common pressures experienced by those working in areas of great social need that were often also multi-ethnic. Bringing people together in a climate such as Steven Croft describes proved to be a great means of encouragement and support. Indeed, it went further, as lay people too began to be involved and the initiative was renamed 'Beyond Survival'. The very names speak of hope and light in the midst of the difficulties and demands of ministry in such areas.

Another actual example of the informal support that is possible, which I have personally found helpful, has been an occasional meeting for clergy responsible for leading larger churches, that is, those with a regular attendance of 200 and over. This has been facilitated by the Church Pastoral Aid Society (CPAS) and gives an opportunity to reflect on both the opportunities and problems that dealing with larger numbers brings. In the past I have also been a part of a network concerned with leading clusters of small rural churches. To these we could add other examples of specialist interest-based groups, chaplaincies or sector ministries that meet on a regular basis. Far more is possible through these means than is often realised and, if they do not exist, it only needs one or two to take an initiative and who knows what might happen!

Along with interpersonal support from fellow clergy, inter-disciplinary support from people in other caring professions working in the same area on common concerns can also be a significant resource. These may include doctors, local councillors, social workers, probation officers, teachers and others as appropriate. Again, my experience tells me that much mutual enrichment and encouragement can come from such people, who are often glad to build relationships with the Church. All this is not to suggest that so much time is spent in meetings and being supported that the actual task of ministry is not carried out. Rather, it is to say that there is much more potential in the peer-group aspect than is often realised, and Andrew Irvine in his book *Between Two Worlds*[6] rightly sees all this as one of the most important solutions to the problems of clergy stress.

Support from the local church

How far can the local church be a support for its minister as well as its members? Indeed, some might want to substitute the word 'should' for 'can'. This is at heart an ecclesiological question – are the clergy a part of the community, or does their calling inevitably mean they are 'apart from': care-givers rather than in need of care? Some specific aspects of this have been explored in Chapters 3 and 4, but my conviction is that while the local church cannot and should not be expected to provide for all needs, if at all possible, clergy should find some support in appropriate ways from the local church community. That of course implies that the clergy are willing to be supported. Sometimes they are the ones who put barriers up. Independent-mindedness rears its head again!

From the mid 1980s to the early 1990s, I worked in the Diocese of Carlisle as Officer for Evangelism. In March 1985 the diocese produced a *Handbook for Church Councils*, in which there was a section on pastoral care exercised via the local church, which ended with some comments on the pastoral care of the clergy. 'It is in the sharing of ministry and pastoral care that clergy and co-workers are able to care most effectively for one another. *The mutual care of the carers must be a prerequisite in effective shared ministry*; without it, there is hardly likely to be effective ministry to others'[7] (emphasis mine).

Clearly there will be some settings where for all kinds of reasons this is not possible, but this Carlisle document sets a vision of collaboration, mutuality and support which clergy can have a right to expect at local church level. I quote again from the same document:

> In the end, the support and help which clergy need is so often no different from the support and help which parishioners seek from them, and the same is true of clergy families. In any parish where there is serious thought given to the possibilities for shared pastoral ministry, all those involved should ask the question: 'are there ways in which we (the laity) can care more effectively for our pastor and his family?'

This support might be demonstrated in a number of different ways: if there is a pattern of daily prayer in the church, it may be through key lay leaders and others supporting that, or through lay people being proactive in asking if there are particular needs for prayer or practical ways in which the clergy's ministry can be helped and made more effective. As mentioned earlier, it could involve the minister seeking out two or three people who will agree to pray specifically for his or her leadership in the church and community. Of course great care is needed in the realm of confidentiality, but this is all about building a climate of openness and trust between minister and congregation. Clergy often speak of isolation and loneliness as a result of their role, and while some of this is inevitable by virtue of being a leader, I believe many would be surprised what might be available if they would only take the risk and ask.

Counselling

In her book *Who Ministers to Ministers?*[8] Barbara Gilbert asks poignantly: 'Clergy and their spouses experience the same kind of joy, pain and brokenness as their parishioners. Where do they turn when faced with personal problems? . . . Do they find the support they need?'

My researches have shown that, generally speaking, crisis care from the hierarchy of the denominations is good, though regular personal pastoral contact is not usually feasible because of the sheer numbers to be cared for. One could parallel this with a local church situation where the minister has a congregation say of 200+. It is both unrealistic and inappropriate for the minister to be in regular pastoral contact with each church member, but what is important is that provision is made, through structures for pastoral care being put in place – in other words, that some kind of delegated pastoral care exists at a number of levels according to need.

One example of the provision of delegated pastoral care is through the availability of counselling for clergy and, where needed, for members of their families. There are moments in anyone's life when they feel they cannot cope for much longer, and professional help needs to be available. Such counselling can provide an opportunity for people to explore their difficulties and problems in a safe and confidential place, in such a way that new insights can be gained into themselves and their situations.

Increasingly, provision of a network of qualified and experienced counsellors is being made, which needs to have the backing of the bishop or his equivalent in the denominational structure, but needs also to be completely independent, without any fear of reporting back.

Although such a service is of particular value and importance at a time of crisis, I believe clergy should also be encouraged to use it whenever they know they need this kind of listening ear, which is both professional and undertaken in the strictest confidence. Counselling of this kind aims to enable people to find their own personal solutions, to recognise their strengths and weaknesses, and to help the individual to take responsibility for his or her own life.

In practical terms, clergy need to have easy access to a list of counsellors, containing information about each one's background and particular skills. A common pattern in many but not all Anglican dioceses seems to be that a counselling service is free for up to six sessions. These should be paid for by the denomination, and part of their annual budget, with further sessions arranged at a rate – which might be subsidised – negotiated with the counsellor concerned. Cost should not be an impediment in seeking this kind of help and support. Some denominations have designated suitably qualified people who co-ordinate this ministry and it seems to me that in these days of stress-related illness of all kinds, a priority needs to be made in this area if it is not already in existence. It is part of the rights clergy have, as one aspect of personal support.

Comments from those who have used a counselling service in one Anglican diocese include:

- 'I see now that my ministry has been an avoidance of loneliness.'
- 'When I get it right for my family I feel I'm failing the parish and vice versa.'

- 'I cannot cope with taking more than four services on a Sunday.'
- 'I feel my ministry should be based on *being* and *holiness* but all the pressure is towards *management* and *success*.'
- 'The Church I have loved and served all my life has no place for my sexuality.'

A very specific aspect of pastoral provision is the help needed when a clergy marriage breaks up. While the divorce rate among the clergy is well below the national average of one in three, it is nonetheless on the increase. Evidence suggests that, whereas in the past many clergy and their wives struggled on in unhappy marriages, in the last twenty years there have been more cases of separation and divorce. This fact is gradually being taken on board by the institutional church, with the establishing of both official measures and better pastoral support in the event of a marriage breakdown.

As well as personal support for both parties and any children involved, there may well need to be practical help and emergency financial provision because the couple are separating. In the Anglican context, support often comes from people called Bishop's Visitors. According to the guidelines for 1996, the job description of the Visitor is that they offer non-judgemental support to the deserted spouse at the time of the breakdown, and for as long as necessary as life is rebuilt.

Broken Rites, an association of divorced and separated clergy wives, works alongside the diocesan Visitors on both a short- and long-term basis. At the time of writing there are over 200 members of Broken Rites, though Christine McMullen, the organisation's secretary, would say this is just the tip of the iceberg. Members around the country offer support on a regional basis, by telephone, e-mail, meetings or local support groups. (At the moment there does not seem to be an equivalent support system for husbands who have been 'deserted'.)

If some such framework is not already in place, a denomination needs to ensure that there are appropriately trained people who can be available, and for this service there should be no charge. Sadly, the Church's track record has not always been good in this area in terms of ongoing care and support and the sense of failure and guilt already felt as a result of relationship breakdown can be further exacerbated.

It also has to be said that clergy and their families are sometimes unwilling to use counselling support networks because of fear that 'showing weakness' may jeopardise their future ministry opportunities. They think they should be able to 'cope'. Yet recognising signs of strain before more serious damage is done, and seeking appropriate help and support is surely a sign of maturity.

This reluctance to seek help may stem from a confusion around the axis of support versus power. This is starkly illustrated by the resignation of the Bishop of Southwark's Director of Clergy Pastoral Care, early in 2001. Following this, a considerable debate was sparked off concerning the role of the bishop in relation to matters of pastoral care. Are bishops primarily managers 'over' or pastors 'for' the clergy in the diocese? Clearly, different bishops will have different priorities, according to their personalities and gifting, but it is important to try and avoid a mismatch of expectations. I believe good management is vital but the framework that provides its legitimacy is that of care for people and everything that makes up their lives. Good pastors will seek to manage people well, and good managers will have a loving care for those in their charge.

Spiritual direction

Although we are ultimately responsible for our own spiritual growth and nurture, it is, I believe, a sign of either arrogance or naivety to think that clergy can manage to survive, let alone be effective in ministry, without some input or guidance from others. Clergy are people who in a very particular way take on board others' needs, questions and struggles specifically on matters of faith, and sometimes life in general. It seems to me nothing short of dangerous for a minister to be so caught up with all this that he or she neglects the need for someone outside both the local and official church structures, to give space both for support and challenge.

Looking back down the centuries, God's methodology has always been to use suitable and appointed representatives to give spiritual direction to leaders or potential leaders of the community of faith. As far back as the era of Moses in the Old Testament, when he was feeling the pressures of changed responsibilities and the seemingly overwhelming demands of leadership, God used his half-converted father-in-law, Jethro, to give him guidance: 'What is this you are doing for the people? Why do you alone sit as judge, while all these people stand around you from morning till evening?' Moses' father-in-law said to him, 'What you are doing is not good. You and these people who come to you will only wear yourselves out. The work is too heavy for you; you cannot handle it alone' (Exodus 18:14–18).

After listening to and observing the stresses and pressures Moses is facing, and having given him a clear analysis of the problem, Jethro then makes a proposal for change that will be beneficial both for Moses and the people for whom he is responsible. He gives nothing less than spiritual direction – and then leaves Moses to work out the implications.

Moving into the New Testament era, one of the unsung heroes of the Acts of the Apostles is Ananias, and his role is to give spiritual direction to the newly converted Saul. The account in Acts 9 makes it clear that this was not a task he relished, because of Saul's reputation as a persecutor and destroyer of Christians. However, Ananias had a key role to bring instruction to this fledgling Christian, to baptise him and to help integrate him into the Christian community in Damascus.

I mention these two examples – and of course there are many others from within the biblical tradition – to illustrate that this concept of spiritual direction is not something peculiar to a particular tradition of the Church, namely Roman or Anglo-Catholic. Nor is it simply for clergy or lay people of certain kinds of temperament or position. It is rather the recognition that as human beings we are so near to ourselves that we need the perspective of others. I love the words of the twelfth-century St Bernard when he said: 'He who essays to teach himself has a fool for a master, and he who pleads his own case in court has a fool for a client.' Similarly, St Augustine said: 'No one can walk without a guide.' From the Reformation era, I note with interest that the great Protestant Reformer, John Calvin, was known as a 'director of souls'.

In the last thirty years, not least as a result of various aspects of the renewing work of the Holy Spirit that the Church has experienced, people from all kinds of backgrounds are finding value in having a spiritual director. This is a potentially vital resource for people in ministry. Indeed, as an example of the changing climate within the Church on this matter, many ordinands emerge from theological colleges of all traditions having already linked up with a spiritual director, or with the expectation that they will find one at the earliest opportunity. That said, however, in my personal researches through surveys conducted at various conferences at which I have spoken, it is rare to find more than 50 per cent of those present who have a spiritual director or equivalent person giving that mixture of support and challenge which is at the heart of the role.

Perhaps that is in part because a mystique can still surround this concept, or because people fear intrusion into their lives. I have even come across the suggestion that it is a sign of weakness to admit the need for input that, as one person has put it, is the combination of 'warm bath and cold shower'. Yet the sense of isolation and low morale that many clergy say they experience today could be greatly helped by some kind of process of spiritual direction.

What then can be the benefits of having a spiritual director? Let me offer two seemingly contrasting definitions from different eras, both of which, however, seem to be saying the same kind of thing: 'Spiritual direction . . . involves the systematic guidance of souls in such a course of interior activities as will remove obstacles to the activities of God within us, and issue in the spiritualising and divinising of the whole life. The soul would thus be able to receive the divine revelation and to respond gladly and readily to every movement of the divine will.'[9] This comes from the Anglo-Catholic 'stable' in the 1950s. More recently, from another part of the Church and most succinctly put, come these words from Rick Lewis, speaking at a conference at Bawtry Hall, Doncaster in 1999: 'Spiritual direction is promoting the work of God in the life of another.'

What is clear from both of these is that in spiritual direction we are talking about something that relates to, is applied to, and must touch the whole of life. It is about all we are in relation to God, ourselves and others – not simply a compartment of life that has on it the label 'spiritual' – and it is about the recognition that obstacles have to be identified and removed. Their removal is of course the work of God, but the identification may come through another person. Whether that person is formally called a spiritual director, a mentor, soul friend, confessor, prayer-partner, guide, companion on the way, or any other term is not the issue. By this I do not mean these are all the same or interchangeable. Rather, what matters is that clergy, if they are to be 'fit to lead' in a changing world, have someone who has the qualities needed to help in the removal of obstacles and bring some clarification and discernment into their lives.

What then might those qualities include? From my own experience of being on the receiving end of spiritual direction on a regular basis for over twenty years, my reading and my own attempts to offer this as a ministry to others, I would identify the following: a person who is open to the Holy Spirit; has experience of life in general, and the Christian journey in particular; is committed to their own learning and growth; has some gifting in the area of discernment; is utterly trustworthy and non-judgemental yet can confront when necessary and, above all, someone who can listen, both to God and to the person receiving direction. As Margaret Guenther has put it, in her book *Holy Listening*,[10] someone who has the gift of 'disinterested loving attention'.

Bearing all this in mind, we can agree with St Gregory, who said: 'The guidance of souls is of all the arts the most excellent.' There is, of course, no such person as the perfect spiritual director. Indeed, as someone once put it: 'A spiritual director who becomes too spiritual is more than a little frightening.'

Happily, most dioceses or the appropriate equivalents in other denominations are waking up to the importance of this aspect of support for clergy. In some instances, lists of names of those who have had some training and experience in spiritual direction are available. Anglican and Roman Catholic religious orders and houses remain a wonderful source of support and expertise in this area, and just asking around among other clergy can provide some helpful pointers.

Ultimately, the aim of spiritual direction is perfection. As St Paul put it in his letter to the Ephesians, writing about the purpose of certain Holy Spirit-inspired ministry gifts, these are given 'to prepare God's people for works of service, so that the body of Christ may be built up until we all reach unity in the faith and in the knowledge of the Son of God, *attaining to the whole measure of the fulness of Christ'* (Ephesians 4:12–13).

Spiritual direction can be one of the resources that assists in this process, moving us in the direction of God to such an extent that we are more open to the work of the Holy Spirit within. This can enable a greater love for and sense of God, and a new experience of love for ourselves and love and concern for others, i.e., the fulfilling of the two great commandments. To me, in the postmodern, post-Christian context in which Christian ministry takes place, there has never been a greater need for the kind of relationship that spiritual direction offers. How exactly this relationship works out will rightly vary from person to person. My own experience of seeing someone four or five times a year, with the knowledge that they can be contacted at other times in extremis seems about right. A flexible approach that ensures the possibility of a dynamic and creative relationship is what matters. Occasionally too there is the need to recognise that a change of director should take place, if for some reason the relationship is no longer being helpful or effective. However things are expressed and worked out, what we are talking about is an approach ideally suited for the twenty-first century where there is the general recognition that many needs are best met through some kind of one-to-one input. As in so many instances, this is not the Church jumping on some kind of contemporary bandwagon – 'everyone's into mentoring these days' – but rather the recognition that 'we were here first'. Some rediscovering and reaffirmation in this area can only be good for the health of the Church and its ministers.

6
Tools for the trade: personal development

a s St Paul makes clear, for the Church to be effective, true to itself and its calling, all must work together for the good of the whole, using their God-given gifts. The role of the clergy as leaders of such collaborative ministry is vital because, contrary to some views of collaborative ministry, the laity are not there to help the clergy to do their job. The clergy are there to help the laity be the church. An Anglican draft document on this subject states:

> The clergy should promote collaborative ministry across the whole range of church life and activity, recognising and affirming lay ministry that already exists and encouraging new ministries, both lay and ordained. They should be ready to assist others in discerning and fulfilling their vocation, and should acknowledge and respect the range of experience amongst the church membership, which can be used for the benefit of all.[1]

The need to grasp these principles has never been more important than it is today, in the changing environment in which clergy are called to minister. Professional expectations are getting higher, the Church is increasingly required to operate within a framework of statutory legislation that has to be understood and adhered to (for example, in child protection matters) and increasingly complex skills are demanded of those in ministry.

There needs also to be continued assessment of training requirements, as well as feedback to theological educators. The last twenty years have seen a healthy shift away from the omni-competent individualist approach that characterised much earlier training and its outworking in pastoral ministry, and that inhibited the principles outlined above. But for those trained in such models, it can come hard to learn new approaches. Even for those committed to a collaborative teamwork approach, I suspect there needs to be a retraining and re-equipping every few years.

Referring again to the values identified by Christopher Spence, outlined in the previous chapter, I now want to focus on the clergy's rights to personal development. In the following chapter, I will deal with the matter of appropriate training in relation to what I believe are some of the key areas of leadership necessary for the twenty-first century.

Continuing Ministerial Education

The phrase 'Continuing Ministerial Education' (CME) would, I suspect, have caused blank looks from earlier generations of clergy. Thinking specifically of the Anglican context, you went to theological college, usually endured rather than enjoyed Post-Ordination Training as a curate for three or four years and were thereby set up for a lifetime's ministry. The author Gerard Kelly challenges such an expectation in today's changing world: 'In a static culture it is enough to learn skills once, perhaps in college, and to dedicate a life to practising them. In a culture re-inventing itself every five to seven years this is untenable . . . To be a leader in the coming decades will mean by definition to be a lifelong learner.'[2]

Although there may still be a residue of the earlier attitudes around, there are some signs of hope, where the importance is being recognised of a commitment to lifelong learning as we respond to this changing context for ministry. This is reflected in the publication during 2001 of *Mind the Gap,*[3] containing a series of recommendations for Church of England dioceses in the area of integrated Continuing Ministerial Education. Within the document is the recognition that in the twenty years since the previous report, *The Continuing Education of the Church's Ministers,* each diocese has developed programmes and provided some funding for the ongoing education and training of ministers.

One of the things that is clear from *Mind the Gap* is that there is no consistent approach to CME. Inevitably, there will need to be variations of practice according to the local context, but among the 25 Recommendations in the Report are the following:

R1: Dioceses preface policy documents with the following state-
     ment: 'The fundamental purpose of Continuing Ministerial
     Education is to equip and develop the Church's ministers in
     order that they may stimulate and enable the whole Church
     to participate more fully in the mission of God in the world.'
R5: 'Over the next two years, each Diocese creates a CME Devel-
     opment Plan (of its own or in regional or ecumenical
     partnership).'

Evidence of the perceived value of CME is seen in practical terms in the way most dioceses allocate a sum of money from their budgets for CME, usually between £100 and £200 per clergy-person each year. Similar provision is made by other denominations. However, beyond this it is possible to identify two overall but contrasting approaches to the delivery of CME – one proactive, the other reactive. The latter style makes infor-mation available about courses, conferences, postgraduate degrees and diplomas but does little or nothing in the way of organising appropriate events. 'It's here if you want it – you must make the going.' I believe this is severely limiting, because in a situation where the internal culture of the church is still coming to terms with recognising the importance of CME, it seems that the people who most need appropriate challenge and stimulus could be the very ones whose CME grants lie unused year after year. This is without considering what input might be helpful in terms of the contemporary Church's role in the world.

In my researches for this book, I came across considerable concern, on the part of bishops and others responsible for ongoing ministerial training, about the resistance factor among clergy to CME. Reasons for this resistance seem to be around issues including relevance, effectiveness of the provision, and timing of events. The degree of episcopal promotion of CME also seems to affect take-up. One bishop identified essentially three types of clergy, whom he described in these terms:

1. The motivated – the majority of whom are at the younger end of the age spectrum, recently ordained, conscious of being on a steep learning curve and of the need to keep up with changes in society and the church.
2. The 'middle-aged' – not necessarily in years but in attitude; content with 'keeping going', fearful in some instances of what is changing around them.
3. The freshly motivated – people ordained after having had a previous career, often high-calibre people who bring both specific areas of expertise and an expectation that 'in-service training' should be of a high quality.

The bishop's comments indicated that the greatest need was to work with the second category, strengthening the role of CME so it becomes something clergy do not want to miss out on.

Obviously, an imposed structure is no better either: 'This is what "we" believe is good for you.' As a reaction to this there is a growing movement to link CME deliberately with ministerial review. In Worcester Diocese for example, following the experience of several residential CME conferences being cancelled owing to lack of interest, a new approach began with CME being linked to ministerial review. Following a review with a senior staff member, a tear-off sheet is sent to the Clergy Training Officer who then discusses the appropriate course of action for ongoing training and development. A similar situation exists in Rochester, where the Director of Ministry and Training will follow up the review section on training outcomes.

Another example of a proactive approach comes from Blackburn Diocese where, through the former Director of Training, personal help and guidance was offered for all clergy. This was done in an informal way and provision was made for a more structured form of consultancy, which included enabling clergy to review their ministry at key points in their career. Bearing in mind clergy operate in an essentially flat career structure, and sometimes get stuck because they have not had the opportunity to review their ministry at key points, it is good to know a number of dioceses now provide something like the above.

In Hereford Diocese, where many clergy operate in isolated rural situations, a CME programme runs jointly for clergy and readers, which is often over-subscribed. It is not uncommon for 80 per cent of the clergy to attend one or more of the 10–15 training events each year. According to the former suffragan Bishop, Dr John Saxbee (now Bishop of Lincoln), the reason for this is that people's isolation means that they value being with others and they also experience the quality of input as being both high and relevant for their ministry. This integrated approach to CME is one of the four principles for CME found in *Mind the Gap*, the other three being to ensure there is a clear rationale, a balance in the programme and ongoing monitoring and evaluation of what is being delivered.

Again in Anglican terms, dioceses vary as to how much of a 'three-line whip' operates as far as CME is concerned. Guildford Diocese, for example, requires clergy to be involved in at least one CME event per year and to use the remainder of their grant for something of their own personal choice. Surely this is a minimum requirement? Every other profession is (rightly) required to ensure that in-service training is offered and completed – can we afford any less a commitment if ministry is to be appropriate and effective? Clearly, however, it must be high quality training and relevant to the participants.

From my research, it seems clergy especially want input at the beginning of this new century on:

- teamwork skills;
- collaborative ministry;
- discerning people's gifts;
- managing change;
- dealing with conflict;
- using new technology;
- interpreting the Bible today;
- the role of the priest in a new century;
- approaches to appropriate styles of worship in the local church;
- responding to the marginalisation of the Church;
- understanding today's 'spiritualities';
- models of church for 'Generation Xers' and the Millennium generation.

I will focus on some of these areas in the next chapter.

A concern I have in hearing and reading about the various in-service training courses on offer is the evident danger of shying away from serious theological content in the programme. *Mind the Gap* also notes the need to do more theological reflection: 'The Church's public ministers need opportunities to engage in learning that will keep them abreast of issues of faith in a post-modern society, Biblical studies, and language and ways of exploring questions of truth in relation to God.'[4] Somehow more work needs to be done on bridging the gap between the theology taught as theory at college and the realities of day-to-day church and parish life. We may be in a 'does it work?' rather than 'is it true?' mode in society, but is that not all the more reason for a fresh approach to apologetics? This is the importance of much current work being done on contextual theology, where theology is not understood primarily as a way of thinking but of living.

I am involved, as part of the teaching team, in a course which seeks to bridge that gap. Based at Cliff College near Sheffield, the Postgraduate Diploma in Leadership, Renewal and Mission Studies seeks to help practitioners from any denomination or stream to reflect theologically on their ministry in a changing world.

Such a concern also lies behind John Reader's work on 'local theology'.[5] This is the account of a church in rural Shropshire seeking to apply its theology to how it expressed its life and engaged in mission. As Robert Warren comments: 'It has done so in a thoroughly postmodern way. Rather than imposing some theological framework ('grand narrative') on the church and community, the church sought to address the issues of the local community – and take time to reflect theologically on the issues. It did so by tackling several projects.'[6] Reader's book *Local Theology* tells the story of how work was done on housing and environmental issues. In approaching these issues, a deliberate choice was made to work from practice to theory, a reversal of the more usual modern Enlightenment approach from theory to practice. Similarly a conscious choice was made to address issues from a spirituality perspective rather than a doctrinal one. Reader's work is full of rich thinking and is of enormous relevance for any minister seeking to engage creatively with today's culture.

Alongside their ongoing ministerial development programmes, most Anglican dioceses have a pattern of a residential clergy conference every two, three or four years, for the inside of a week. Other denominations have similar opportunities for coming together in a wider context than the local. As well as building the sense of value and belonging referred to in an earlier chapter, at their best these conferences can be important opportunities for reflection, learning and growth. As a variant to this pattern, one diocese ran a series of smaller conferences in the 1990s which enabled groups of clergy to get to know one another better, while engaging with important concerns in ministry and mission over a three-day period.

Ministerial review

The present ordination service from the Church of England's Alternative Service Book includes within it a section that speaks not only of an expectation of trust and commitment on the part of those called into such ministry, but also a right kind of accountability. 'In the name of the Lord we bid you remember the greatness of the trust now to be committed to your charge, about which you have been taught in your preparation for this ministry. You are to be messengers, watchmen and stewards of the Lord.'[7]

Similar expectations are expressed in ordination services found in other denominations, and the aim of ministerial review, however it is conducted, is to provide a regular opportunity for those ordained to reflect on their calling and the outworking of their ministry. It is part of the recognition that ordination is a key moment of response to vocation, but is by no means the end of it. As a diocesan handbook puts it: 'Rather, as a person's ministry is offered and the practical realities of Christian leadership and service are worked out, the sense of God's calling is likely to deepen, to mature and, from time to time, to open up in new directions.'[8]

The draft *Guidelines for the Professional Conduct of the Clergy* reflects a growing understanding of the importance of this: 'The bishop or his trained representative should also undertake a regular review and appraisal of each clergyperson's work that should be clearly linked into the purposeful development of the individual's ministry, within the context of the needs of the Church.'[9]

Whatever the precise methodology, most of the 43 dioceses of the Church of England along with other mainstream denominations now have in place some kind of ministerial review scheme. In different ways these seek to make real the theological partnership between the local church and the ministry of the whole/universal Church. Some are compulsory while others are voluntary. There has been, on the part of some clergy, a reluctance to see the value of such a process – indeed a tendency on the part of some to find it an intrusion on their ministry. Part of this has been because of the word 'appraisal', which was in more common use a few years ago. (Appraisal, as used in other work contexts, is often about monitoring performance, remuneration and career prospects.) Some clergy were angry at such a concept or felt it inappropriate to measure ministry in this way. Others were fearful that they might not 'come up to scratch'. The issues are not simply a matter of semantics, but the word 'review' speaks more of a process of encouragement and support, rather than threat, and there is a growing recognition (as the above quote from the ordinal certainly makes clear) that clergy must live responsibly with their vocation – responsibly to God, to themselves and the people for whom they are pastorally responsible.

To quote the Rochester *Ministry Review Handbook*: 'The 'Ministry Review scheme provides us with the regular opportunity to consider our calling and the practice of our own ministry. This is one of the ways in which we can become more open to the renewal of our own spirituality and our competence as servants and leaders of the church we serve.'[10]

Given that there are various possible approaches to ministerial review, it seems to me that the word *regular* is key in the process. At least once a year, each minister should have such an opportunity to reflect on their ministry, their spirituality, their personal lives and future development. Some review schemes also include questions on matters of personal and family life. Provided it is set up in the appropriate way, the experience of ministerial review should be nothing other than beneficial, as people experience respect, being heard, acceptance, affirmation – an appropriate mix of support and challenge.

What many Anglican dioceses are now doing is offering a three-year cycle, where one year's review is with a bishop, the second with an archdeacon or other senior staff member, and the third is a 'peer review' or the opportunity to meet with a lay consultant. The first two of these may well be helped by a questionnaire, which is sent out in advance of the review, covering the key areas of the review. The responses to this, and anything in writing, need to be kept confidential between the minister and the reviewer, except for particular training needs which may have been identified. If the reviewer is not the bishop, there may also be particular information he may need for the present and future well-being and development of the minister. However, clarity on what is passed on and appropriate permission being given are essential for the review system to work effectively and with trust at its heart. Some dioceses add on a further, and I believe healthy and helpful element, whereby the bishop or archdeacon also spends time on the day of the review in the local church setting, seeing the outworking of a person's ministry at first hand and having the opportunity to meet informally with churchwardens and the Church Council to discuss the life and ministry of the church.

When it comes to peer review, guidelines are agreed, and what often happens is that clergy choose a peer reviewer from a list of names. It is vital that those working as reviewers have had some suitable training beforehand. The peer reviewer's role is to help the minister coming to them to see and evaluate their work more clearly. It involves active listening with respect and delight, enabling an articulation of hopes and fears, joys and frustrations. Peer reviewers may be clergy or lay people. Sometimes, to balance the other kinds of review, there could be an advantage in seeing a lay person. What goes on in the peer review is totally confidential, unless something is clearly and specifically agreed otherwise.

Another model, now used for example in the Methodist Church, is that of 'accompanied self-appraisal'. This takes place twice a year and the chairman of the district only knows that it has taken place, and not the details of the conversation. Members can choose who 'accompanies' them, from a list of trained people. The idea here is to ensure that all the key areas of ministry are discussed at some point within a three- or four-year period.

Review schemes seem to work best when senior staff of the denomination are themselves also involved in a ministerial review process. Thus, in a number of Anglican dioceses, the diocesan bishop will review his senior staff, while he in turn is reviewed by another bishop or someone under the scheme run by the national Bishops' Officer for Training. That review report is then sent to the Archbishop of Canterbury.

Stages of ministry and change of responsibilities

In addition to what I have described in the preceding section, I believe many denominations could benefit from a scheme such as that utilised by the Church of Scotland. Within this scheme, ministers are invited to attend three-day conferences to reflect on their ministry past, present and future, after eighteen months, five, eight and fifteen years in post. This is funded by the denomination and aims to help clergy to understand changes in society, to meet with others in similar circumstances and with similar experience of ministry and to think *without pressure* about where their ministry is going and whether or not a move or change of direction would be appropriate. Surely it would not be beyond the bounds of possibility for most denominations to set up something similar and thereby further help the morale and sense of value of the clergy? Too often such discussions only take place when something specific comes up, and sometimes clergy seem to move from one place to another without an opportunity to stop and reflect. The report *Mind the Gap*, in Recommendation 15, shows an awareness of the importance of such provision: 'We recommend that agreed expectations are used by minister and CME or ministerial review consultant as a guide in drawing up a ministerial development statement immediately prior to a point of transition in ministry.'[11]

Linked to this is the importance of offering 'changes of responsibility' conferences. In no other profession would people be allowed to move, without any training or preparation, into new areas of responsibility where they have had little or no previous experience. Consider, for example, the pressure on someone moving from being an assistant in a leafy suburban parish to having pastoral charge of either an inner-city church or eight rural communities. Even more starkly, I have known people moving into specialised areas of ministry such as evangelism or social responsibility with little or no training or induction.

The five key milestones of ministerial development seem to me to be:

- post-ordination;
- first pastoral charge;
- new post/change of responsibility;
- mid-service;
- pre-retirement.

The opportunity to stop, reflect and identify development needs at these points could make a huge difference to clergy's morale and long-term effectiveness.

Sabbaticals

If the recognition of the importance of ongoing ministerial training and ministerial review are relatively recent innovations in most denominations, so is the possibility of a sabbatical. However, there is an increasing recognition, as Andrew Irvine writes, that 'the hectic pace of today's world and the forced productivity of both soil and soul make this ever more a necessity.'[12]

Mindful of this increased pace of life, the need for a commitment to lifelong learning and a decreasing number of clergy available to share an increasing level of pastoral responsibility, many denominations are now encouraging such time out for clergy. Perhaps it would be better to describe this as a rediscovery rather than an innovation, because the opening pages of Scripture witness to a rhythm in the process of creation, which is intended to be reflected in the life of humanity (Genesis 2:2). This weekly 'gift' is supplemented by the sabbath year concept in Leviticus 25, as far as the land is concerned.

The purpose of sabbatical time is essentially fourfold: for reflection, re-creation, study, and personal and spiritual nurture. As we have noted, the busyness of much current church life and ministry means there is often insufficient time for these elements to be present, and a sabbatical can be both a timely gift in itself and the opportunity to refocus with new priorities for ongoing ministry. *Mind the Gap* puts it this way, in Recommendation 22: 'All licensed ministers (lay and stipendiary) should be given the opportunity of a sabbatical i.e.: a time of rest, renewal and recreation, whether or not a financial contribution is made by the Diocese.'[13]

Sabbaticals vary in length and frequency, but the most common pattern is to make them available every seven or ten years, usually lasting about three months. Help with financing sabbaticals is increasingly being built into diocesan or their equivalent bodies' budgets, and help to fund travel and study can often be found through various trusts and charities.

Having benefited from a first sabbatical after 26 years in ordained ministry, I now wonder why it is, when they are available, still comparatively few clergy take up the opportunity. I think it is because there are both practical and attitudinal issues to be overcome. On the practical front, sabbaticals may need to be given a higher profile by the church authorities. At an individual level, there may be particular family or local church issues to be taken into consideration. My personal experience of waiting so long for a sabbatical often seemed to hinge around feeling it was not an ideal time from that point of view. In reality there is no ideal time but, acknowledging that some times are of course better than others, I realised it was primarily an attitudinal issue I was dealing with. 'I'd love to have this "time out", but how will I cope with being "out of role"? Can I trust others to take responsibility in my absence? Might they actually be more effective than me? How will the church cope? What might I discover or rediscover about myself that has been buried beneath the busyness of ministerial and family life?' It is very easy for clergy over a period of time to find their security in their role rather than in who they are in Christ – as someone has put it, to have no more than a 'satisfactory working relationship' with God. These are attitudinal issues at the personal level.

Then there are fears, real or imaginary, that others, particularly in the local church, will resent or misunderstand the sabbatical: 'Why should s/he have this when the rest of us never get a break?' In this regard, I came across some very disturbing comments from clergy responsible for chaplaincies in the Anglican Diocese in Europe – and this may apply to other denominations or traditions where the clergy are paid directly from the local congregation. More than one chaplain told me that his local church council was happy for him to have a sabbatical as long as he footed the bill for a locum in his place. This was in addition to funding the sabbatical itself.

It perhaps needs challenge from, as well as support on the part of, the denominations to help congregations understand the purpose of sabbaticals. This might include the provision of a locum replacement for the minister, and financial support and guidance on planning and using sabbaticals effectively. Furthermore, I believe clergy can help themselves more by being less apologetic to and more open with their congregations in this matter. One approach might be to say 'In order for me to be the best possible minister I can be for you in the ministry and mission to which God has called me; in order to ensure there is greater depth in my own personal spirituality and healthy and growing relationships in my family, I need a sabbatical.' It is about communicating that this is in everyone's interests. I have to say that quite a few people in my own congregation, as well as in my family, have commented positively on the difference between post-sabbatical and pre-sabbatical man!

Before leaving this area, from both personal experience and observation of others I would want to say three things. First, the modelling of sabbatical leave by those in the leadership of the denominations is important both for them and also in sending the right signals to clergy and members of congregations. Second, there needs to be a balance created for the sabbatical period. I have already mentioned the fourfold purpose of reflection, re-creation, study, and personal and spiritual nurture. For most of us, this will not happen without some planning. When I was enthusing about the plans I had for reading, writing and travel in my sabbatical, my spiritual director wisely said, 'Don't replace one kind of work with another. Build in a balance of study and research, rest and relaxation, time with the family, visits to other churches for worship where you have no leadership responsibilities.' Third, think carefully about the re-entry after the sabbatical. A wise older clergyman, speaking out of his own mistake of ending his sabbatical with an eight-day retreat, said, 'If you're going to have that as part of the experience, do it at least a week before you return to responsibilities.' Having been out of action for three months, ending with eight days of silence made, for him, a bumpy re-entry.

Certainly my sabbatical experience enabled me to refocus attention from task-orientation to finding fresh intimacy with God, which I believe has in turn helped me to re-establish a more balanced identity. So if you are reading this as an ordained person who has been in ministry a while and never had a sabbatical, is it time to set some wheels in motion? If the immediate thought that comes to mind is 'Can I afford to?' – whether in terms of time, finance or other practicalities – it might be better to ask a different question: 'For everyone's sake, including my own, can I afford not to?' If on the other hand you are a lay person, with or without leadership responsibilities in your church, and are concerned for your clergy's well-being, why not suggest the idea in an appropriate way, as a practical expression of that concern.

In her book *At Ease with Stress*[14] Wanda Nash reminds us that wholeness means caring for all of ourselves – body, mind and spirit. Her sharp challenge to those who feel they have too many demands is, honestly, how much of this 'over' demand comes out of my choice? From pride and ineffective relationships or unhelpful work patterns perhaps? The more demands there are, the more we must both take charge of ourselves and be recharged in appropriate ways, including input to enable both a more professional and more sustainable ministerial lifestyle.

7
Tools for the trade: ministerial skills

Teamwork skills

'Leadership and team working are closely linked. Leaders tend to create teams, and teams look for leaders' (John Adair).[1]

If we again look to Jesus as our inspiration, we see that he chose to build the Church and advance the Kingdom of God by means of a call to volunteers – those first disciples – and what is also clear is that he called them into a team. We see something similar as the Acts of the Apostles describe the growth and development of the fledgling Church. It is interesting to note that, of the disciples whom Jesus called, some were used to teamwork while others were not. Fishing on the Sea of Galilee certainly called for teamwork, between the boats as well as among the crew of each boat (cf. Mark 1:16). Others in the original band of twelve seem very much to have been individuals.

As then, so now: some people are, by temperament and/or training, 'team people', while others are by nature 'lone-rangers', individualists. However, one bishop, when asked what he would do if he or his diocese received a substantial cash windfall, responded: 'Use it to train and equip clergy to work collaboratively with each other and with their congregations. I would want to do it sufficiently thoroughly for it to be a positive rather than a threatening experience.' He then went on to describe how an Outward Bound Centre had offered facilities, at a much-reduced rate, for a ten-day course for clergy on teamwork, problem-solving and the management of change. Those who went on it apparently described the experience as life-changing, and continued to meet together from time to time afterwards, as they assimilated the learning and reflected on how they were operating differently in their ministries as a result of the course.

In most theological colleges, certainly in the past, the 'lone-ranger', individualist style has been taught and subsequently modelled in local churches. There is evidence of a change for the better now, as seen in a document produced by the Church of England. Stephen Croft comments: 'In 1993, the Church of England published revised criteria for the selection for ministry and for the first time included a section on leadership and collaboration, in response to the perceived needs of church and society.'[2] For those who have been in ministry some considerable time, old habits can die hard. However, apart from the principle involved, that it makes for a healthier church and ministry when teamwork and collaboration exist, there are also pragmatic reasons why this needs to be understood and taught afresh. With fewer clergy on the ground, learning to work co-operatively rather than competitively within and between churches has never been more important, if clergy are not to burn out, and the Church's effectiveness is not to be further marginalised.

At a superficial level, it could appear that Jesus' call and the expectation of instantaneous obedience suggests a very autocratic, non-collaborative style of leadership, and as a result a certain kind of relationships, such that 'teamwork' hardly seems an appropriate description! However, 'Follow me', I believe, is more of an invitation than an order, not least as we observe that people could and did say 'no' to being part of the team. Indeed, as the gospels unfold and the cost of the call became too much for some, at least in the wider circle of the disciples, we read that: 'From this time many of his disciples turned back and no longer followed him. "You do not want to leave too, do you?" Jesus asked the Twelve. Simon Peter answered him, "Lord, to whom shall we go? You have the words of eternal life. We believe and know that you are the Holy One of God" ' (John 6:66–69).

This sense of invitation, and the freedom at any point to leave, is important to note. It challenges any notion that blind, unquestioning obedience has anything to do with a true understanding of Christian leadership and teamwork. If we turn to the farewell discourses in John (chapters 13 to 17) we see this powerfully illustrated in Jesus' words: 'No longer do I call you servants, I call you friends' (John 15:15). Jesus' style is about partnership, not a 'top-down', hierarchical approach. St Paul develops this too in his writings, as evidenced by the fact that he refers to thirteen different people as *synergoi* – fellow workers, partners in the Gospel. This is not one person 'over' others but people working in partnership towards a common goal.

Leadership in this sense is about a journey. Indeed the Anglo-Saxon words from which 'lead', 'leader' and 'leadership' derive are travelling, movement words. A leader was one who, in one form or another, showed the way on a common journey. Like leadership, 'team' is also associated with journeys. In early English usage it often referred to groups of animals united together and driven by a 'teamster', with the aim of moving something from one point to another, or a flock of wild birds flying in formation. Over time, in the English language, the word 'team' came to mean any example of people coming together and working for some common purpose, as in a sports team. Thus, a team is a number of people associated with joint activity, working together.

What are the implications of this for the minister seeking to offer effective leadership and enable good teamwork in the twenty-first century? John Finney puts it starkly: 'When a leader says "I can do it better myself", he is criticising his own failure in selecting and developing the gifts of others.'[3]

In broad terms, the task of leadership has been described as being threefold: to provide vision/articulate the task; to establish teamwork; to motivate and develop individuals.[4] *Vision,* according to the Oxford Dictionary, is 'all that comes into view when the eyes are turned in the same direction'. The vision, which may be of a 'big picture' to do with the whole direction of the Church, or something very specific, for example, 'to develop detached youth work on a local authority housing estate', needs to be articulated and communicated clearly and effectively to everyone affected by it. Then it needs to be translated into a set of attainable goals and objectives. These are like milestones or staging posts towards which those directly involved in the process of making the vision a reality can work.

What then is the *team* in this context? Again from the Oxford Dictionary: a team is 'a group of people who share common objectives and who will work together to achieve them'. It is about individuals working together and, through their different gifting, achieving more together than they would alone. Teams, like other organisms, have a recognisable pattern of growth, which can be observed and described. Sadly, teamwork in the church context often does not reach its full potential because of a failure to take this pattern into account. There are four commonly recognised stages of team development: forming, storming, norming and performing.

- *Forming:* when the group or team first forms, or comes together, the members are like hesitant swimmers, dipping their toes in the water. There is a lot of uncertainty around and no established way of working together. Relationships tend to be rather superficial.
- *Storming:* as people realise what is involved, there can be clashes of expectations. This can lead to some panic, like non-swimmers jumping in at the deep end. This is often a difficult time for the team and its leaders, when disagreements surface and conflicts arise, as the group endeavours to sort itself out.
- *Norming:* as people get used to working together, members stop struggling and start helping each other to stay afloat. There is more cohesion and acceptance of common problems, and recognition of each other's strengths.
- *Performing:* the team has now reached a stage where there is

acceptance of one another; people feel more comfortable with each other and are clear about their purpose. It could be said that they are now ready for synchronised swimming!

It is important to note that if membership of the team changes, or if the team encounters major problems, then they may need to go through the cycle again. Simply because conflict has been faced and dealt with in the past, it does not mean it will not recur in the future.

Whether in a clergy team, group ministry, a local church leadership team, a church council, elders' or deacons' group, understanding these stages and what is going on above and beneath the surface can make an enormous difference, both to the achievement of the vision and the development of individuals within the team. Part of the leader's task is to help the team address issues that may arise at each stage.

The third important aspect of the leader's task is *developing and caring for individuals*, so that they are happy, motivated and effective. This includes setting goals and targets, discussing with people how they are doing and giving encouragement, feedback and constructive criticism where necessary. Further perspectives on this are considered in the next section on volunteers.

Effective teams maintain a creative tension between the vision, the needs of individuals and the team dynamics. Clergy and other leaders in the Church need a high level of awareness and ongoing training in the skills required to manage this complex process. It makes the challenge even greater, that none of these areas exist in isolation from the others. They interact and overlap. Furthermore, the sense of team is not built by giving equal attention to all the elements throughout the life of the team. Recognition of what should take precedence at any given time is crucial to the process of effective team-building. So for example, in the early stages of building the team the leader's role has a higher profile, as they invite, recruit and select people and then, consciously or unconsciously, model the values by which the team will operate. What matters is not so much what the first decisions are but how they are made. If most contributions come from relatively few people, a pattern will be established. If meetings start late, it quickly becomes acceptable practice for people to be late.

Returning to the gospels and Jesus with his 'team', we see in the first nine chapters of St Luke's gospel, up to the sending out of the seventy, a strong focus on Jesus. During this time the disciples watched and learned. They began to understand his ways of doing things. Clearly also there was a high degree of personal commitment to Jesus on the part of the disciples. In the next phase, 'results' became more important, as the disciples also engaged in ministry. The final phase, as described in the Upper Room discourses of John 13—17, sees the emphasis on the dynamics of the team, with the aim that, after Jesus has returned to the Father, the disciples together should achieve more than they could as a group of individuals.

Where teams sometimes fall down is in rushing towards that third stage, without going through the other two. If values are not identified and expressed, it is a recipe for conflict. As an example, in the staff team which I currently lead, on a regular basis and certainly when there is any change of personnel, we articulate and agree the values by which we seek to operate, in the local church context. Our current list comprises:

- lead a 'spiritually surrendered' life;
- model a 'whole-life commitment';
- maintain an infectious, optimistic, enthusiastic attitude;
- commit to honest communication;
- manage boundaries;
- honour and value volunteers – the church is built through them;
- keep one eye on eternity;
- depend totally on God.

Having looked at the theory behind the dynamics of team leading and the process of team building and teamwork, it might be helpful to illustrate what this might look like in practice, for example in a typical situation such as a staff team meeting. Since the beginning of a meeting lays the foundations for what follows, before getting on to the agenda proper, two things are helpful: first, to allow space and time for prayer – the conscious recognition of God's presence and the need of his wisdom and guidance; second, to give time for each person present to share something positive. Examples might be: something good that has happened recently, what they are encouraged by in their work, what is keeping them hopeful, or what they are learning about themselves. In a larger group, this may be better done in pairs or triads. The point of this sharing is that before the formal agenda is embarked on, equality is established by each person having the opportunity to speak, and a positive tone is set for the meeting. Although there may be initial resistance to this (see *forming* and *storming*!) it can raise the quality of thinking and discussion to a new level. It will also assist with conflict resolution and decision-making. Agreeing other values, such as people being able to speak without interruption, and adopting the discipline of saying something positive about a proposal before criticising it, can also transform the atmosphere and effectiveness of a team meeting. Endings are important too, and giving a few minutes at the end to review what has been accomplished and what has been valued can enable people to leave the meeting feeling inspired, encouraged, hopeful, motivated and better connected with other members of the team.

As Bryn Hughes says: 'Building a team takes time – it's just whether you see it as a waste of time or an investment. Generally the returns on the investment are actually greater productivity as well as higher morale, a lower turnover of membership and less conflict.'[5]

Managing and enabling change

I have heard many versions of the story about the Anglican churchwarden who had been in post for over forty years. When a visitor to the church commented that he would have witnessed many changes during that time, his reply was: 'Yes, and I've opposed every one of them!'

Anyone in a leadership role – and the church context is no

exception – knows something of the power of resistance to change. Perhaps as a reaction to a world where everything seems to be changing rapidly, that resistance can increase rather than decrease. It seems important, therefore, if the Church is to be effective in its ministry and mission in a changing world, that clergy understand the principles and practice that lie behind enabling and managing change.

The first point to be grasped is that 'both environmental necessity and theological imperative point to the inevitability of change.'[6] An organism that does not adapt to changes in its environment will die. The Christian Scriptures make clear that the people of God are called to be a pilgrim people, a people on the move, with all that this implies. Whether that is Abraham (Genesis 12:1), Moses (Exodus 3:7–8), Jesus himself (Mark 1:16–18) or the early Christian leaders (Acts 1:8; 11:17), the message is clear – to be a leader involves enabling change. What is also clear is that situations of both growth and decline pose the necessity for change, and as statistics suggest, it is the latter which provides the greatest challenge in our country at the present time. 'We do not advocate change for the sake of change. We see change as the condition of survival.'[7]

Nonetheless, change for individuals, groups, organisations and communities is often not an easy process either to enable or to live with. Any proposal for change is likely to generate a wide range of reactions, from the wildly enthusiastic to the utterly resistant. Thought and skill are therefore needed, on the part of those who are in leadership positions, to create, manage and respond to these processes of change.

Reactions to change will be affected by a number of factors. These include:

- *personality* – some people thrive on change, while others find it fundamentally threatening;
- *context* – is it secure and positive or is this latest change the last straw? Understanding the history of people and places is important because roots go deep;

- *trust* – what degree of trust is there in the vision and abilities of those in leadership who are proposing change?
- *manner of implementation* – what does this have to say about what has gone before or presently exists?
- *effect on individuals* – is the proposed change consistent with people's values and beliefs? Will it involve risk-taking? Is it threatening to their status? Is it breaking new ground?

As well as considering these factors, it can be useful to bear in mind certain guidelines – stages that are necessary along the way. Moving towards change is not usually a neat and tidy process, and some conflict is inevitable. Indeed, it may be necessary. However, unhelpful conflict can be minimised by wise and prayerful leadership, with attention being given to understanding the change process.

The first and most important task is *to assess the need for and create a climate for change*. Holding before people a vision of what could and should be under God is not sufficient. Change will not take place until there is enough discontent with the status quo, and people are motivated enough to do something about it. As someone has put it, in terms of the Old Testament Exodus narrative: 'People need to see the Promised Land and be fed up with Egypt!'

A helpful tool at this stage is to think of the process of change in terms of an equation:

$C \ f \ D + V + F \geqslant £$

where C (Change) is a function of:

D = the level of dissatisfaction / discontent with the current situation, plus

V = a vision of the desired future situation, plus

F = clarity about the first steps that can be taken towards change, all of which must be greater than or equal to £ = the perceived cost involved (be that financial, practical or emotional).

David Cormack has put it like this: 'The amount of change experienced in any situation is dependent on the level of discontent + the degree of clarity of the common vision + the knowledge of the first steps + the energy available. The sum of these elements must be greater than the cost of change.'[8]

The following diagram might also help to explain, in particular, how the *timing of change* is all important:

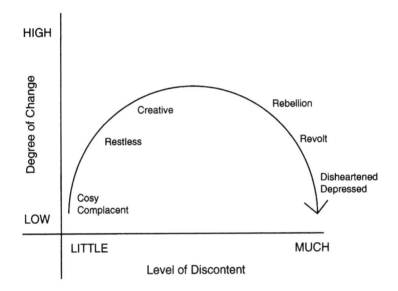

Whether it is major change affecting the whole life and direction of a local church, a diocese, a district or an entire denomination, it is clear that recognising 'where we are on the graph' is crucial to effective management of the process. For example, if people are feeling too comfortable, there will be no momentum for change. If the optimum points are missed, too much discontent can lead to people feeling disheartened or depressed, and eventually to rebellion or distrust of the leadership and a consequent difficulty in enabling change.

Having begun to assess the need for change, and 'taken the temperature' in terms of the climate for change, *building a leadership team*, with a mixture of gifts, skills, ages and temperaments, is vital. Particular abilities to look for in choosing team members are people of vision, those with gifts of discernment and wisdom, and people who have a proven track record of credibility in terms of character and action in the context where change is to take place. Taking time in discussion with other leaders and developing a sense of trust among them will in turn produce unity of purpose and a greater likelihood of changes being accepted.

Consultation and communication form the next key stage in an effective change process. The biggest mistake I have made, and I see evidence of this among other church leaders, is to under-communicate. It has been said that when we sense we are into overkill in communication terms, we are probably doing just about enough! This is in large part because people latch on to the idea of change at different rates. Everett Rodgers[9] is credited with describing people in these ways: the 'innovators' – those who have the ideas – on average about 2 per cent of people; the 'early adopters' – those who latch on pretty quickly to new ideas – about 14 per cent of people; the 'early majority' – about 34 per cent of people, who will take to a new idea when they see others adopting it; the 'late majority' – again some 34 per cent of people, who will only take on board a new idea when they realise that if they don't, they will be left behind; and the 'last adopters' – 16 per cent of the total, who remain sceptical and suspicious of change.

Bearing all this in mind, the key elements of good communication include informing and consulting as widely as possible. To do this, use multiple forms of communication – congregational meetings; smaller group meetings; one-to-one conversations; visual presentations; written information via newsletters, magazine articles and personal notes to people. Use different voices to reflect the team nature of the approach to change. Pay particular attention to objectors, listening carefully to them, trying to understand why they are objecting and giving plenty of time to take note of their views. It is important to remember that change may be occurring in many different places in people's lives, and a reluctance to embrace change may be an indication of a general sense of instability rather than a real antagonism to the particular changes being proposed. Once decisions are made, again keep people informed as to the implications.

When implementing decisions, I have often found that a trial period or time of experimentation can be very helpful. For example, I was involved in managing a change process some years ago which, after all due discussion and consultation, resulted among other things in a decision being taken to adopt a new pattern of Sunday worship. Having presented the way forward, I indicated that this would initially be for a three-month period, after which time it would be reviewed. Following that review, and after making a number of modifications, the experiment continued for another year, when we had a further congregational meeting to assess the effectiveness (or otherwise) of the changes made. Only then was the proposed worship pattern adopted as something appropriate for the medium to long term.

The illustration points to the final key element in the process – *anchoring* the change into the culture and keeping it in place. By culture, I mean the shared values and norms of the local context ('the way we do things around here'). New developments are fragile and need a period of consolidation. However, my experience suggests that as people begin to see the benefits of the change or changes, they in turn change, coming to accept the new situation. Then the whole thing becomes more secure. Eventually, what has changed will become the status quo – 'normal'.

As I bring this section to a close, it may be worth drawing attention to two other factors to watch out for. First, too much change all at once can be overwhelming. The ability of a church to cope with change grows with positive experience. When morale is low, people are reluctant to 'think big'. So, although the minister, church council and others in leadership may have a long-term vision, in some situations decisions may have to be restricted to what can be accomplished successfully over a short period.

Second, a change that is 'more of the same' is easiest to handle. Discontinuities – which are sometimes necessary or inevitable, whether that is in the form of a change of leadership, a new vision or a new approach – are the most difficult and generally need more time from intention to implementation. (A useful strategy in some instances may be to run the new alongside the existing for a period of time, to avoid this discontinuity.)

It does not surprise me at all that clergy have indicated that this area of their leadership is one where they often feel ill-equipped. Managing and enabling change can be costly and painful, and when resistance or opposition rear their heads, the temptation to withdraw or become inflexible or angry with those who disagree can be great. But when enough attention is given to the process and the emotional effects of change, it can be an exciting and invigorating process for all concerned. The bottom line has to be that the change will better enable the ministry and mission entrusted to the Church. Linked to this is the recognition that whenever there is change (positive or negative, desired or not) something is lost and the cost of that letting-go process, for individuals and the Church as a whole, must be acknowledged and honoured.

Volunteering and vocation

I identify this as a particular area where clergy need training and support for two reasons. First, as Bill Hybels, Senior Pastor of Willow Creek Community Church in Chicago put it, the Church is a 'volunteer intensive organisation'.[10] As I have already noted, Jesus began and built the church this way, from the call of his first disciples, and this is how it continues.

Second, in contemporary society not only the Church, but many other voluntary organisations, societies, political parties and trades unions are having problems with volunteering. At one time, particularly in more middle-class areas, there was a cultural expectation that working as a volunteer was 'something you do' as part of being a responsible citizen and member of the community. Now, the stresses and demands of work or family pressures often mean less time is available for such activity. For young people, who might have taken a gap year and worked as a volunteer lay assistant in a local church, perhaps receiving an honorarium, there are now more pressures to get quickly into the job market – not least to pay off student loans and debts.

Also, they are more sophisticated about what resonates as being worthwhile, or is seen to be 'cool' – and often the Church does not figure too highly on that scale!

The National Centre for Volunteering, in its booklet *The Recruitment Guide*[11] published in 1999, refers to some research that produced a 'wish list' for what young people want from volunteering, which is summarised under the acronym FLEXIVOL:

- flexibility – the most important factor, in terms of time and commitment;
- legitimacy – they need a favourable image of volunteering;
- ease of access – many young people do not know how to volunteer or whom to contact;
- 'xperience' – young people want relevant, useful experience and the chance to learn new skills;
- incentives – stress the tangible outcomes of volunteering; what's in it for them;
- variety – in terms both of the type of work and the level of commitment;
- organisation – volunteering needs to be efficient but informal;
- laughs – volunteering must be fun!

Add to this the 'pic'n'mix' approach to life that means long-term commitment to anything is less likely, volunteering being just one among other options available, and it is no wonder the Church like other organisations is now struggling to recruit and retain volunteers.

At this point it is essential to acknowledge that there is an important sense in which the Church is also different from other organisations. Indeed, at its heart, it is an organism. As St Paul makes clear in his letters, the Holy Spirit gives gifts within the body of Christ to enable its life, ministry and mission. Key passages that speak of this are 1 Corinthians 14, Romans 12 and Ephesians 4. Furthermore, in the first letter of Peter, chapter 4, he speaks of Christians being good stewards of God's grace, using whatever gifts God has entrusted to them. Part of a true understanding of collaborative ministry is the process of discernment of these gifts by the Church's leaders. My experience is that as people become part of the local Christian community, various strategies for discerning gifts can be put into place, for example by means of some kind of 'spiritual-gift awareness' course, of which there are a number in existence.

That said, the Church and its leaders have to address the changing situation in which we find ourselves in a creative way.

Asking the right questions and with the right motives is the essential starting point. It is no good seeking to recruit volunteers if we do not know exactly why we want them, what they will be expected to do, how they will be supported and what procedures of selection and training are appropriate. If this sounds somewhat bureaucratic, think about the alternative that is often in evidence. A need or vacancy arises in some area of the Church's life; mention of it is made in the church notice sheet or by someone desperately appealing for help. Eventually someone might agree to take on the responsibility, either out of guilt or at least to ensure that the particular area of church life doesn't fold up. However, they may not have sensed any call from God and it is likely to be all duty and no joy. Once the vacancy has been filled, the minister is often so relieved that he or she moves straight on to sorting out the next area of need, and so there is no sense of ongoing support or offer of appropriate training. No wonder, as Steven Croft has put it, 'the impression [is given] that the congregation is run by a handful of hard-pressed volunteers perpetually on the brink of exhaustion.'[12]

So what strategies might help when a vacancy occurs? First, the question 'is this task essential?' should be asked. Some tasks are continued when they should be stopped because needs and priorities have changed. (The Church is notorious for continuing things that should stop!) Perhaps the role needs to be modified and the vacancy actively gives a creative opportunity for this to happen. Maybe the role could be divided or shared out in a different way.

Second comes the discernment of the skills and gifts needed to fulfil this particular task. This is about discerning both spiritual gifting and practical aptitude. Clergy can sometimes be more concerned to get anyone at all into a role, rather than the person with the appropriate gifts and skills. In some instances it is advisable to try and identify a shortlist of people who may have the necessary qualities and then approach them directly. It has been my practice to do this especially in the more sensitive areas of church life such as the healing ministry.

Third, the decision needs to be made as to how long the person is going to be expected to fulfil the task. Churches are notorious for having a 'life-sentence' approach when it comes to volunteers. We will all have known people who took on leading children's work 'on a temporary basis to help out' 25 years ago and are still doing it! This is not healthy or respectful of the volunteer concerned and it also sends warning signals out to the congregation, which will inhibit volunteering in other areas. It can be helpful to have a trial period for say six months, with the opportunity then to review the effectiveness of the appointment.

Fourth, people want clear information. A simple job description, with what the task entails and how much time commitment is expected, gives people the information needed to help them come to an informed decision.

Fifth, it needs to be made plain what support is being offered for the task. Obviously the kind of support will depend on the nature of the work and the individual needs of the volunteers themselves. So, for example, someone on the church cleaning rota will need a different kind of support and supervision from someone heading up the church's healing prayer ministry, themselves in turn overseeing a number of volunteers. One is not intrinsically more important than the other – but they demand different levels and methods of support. Also, if something goes wrong, is it clear to whom the volunteer should look for support?

Finally, for example in areas of ministry such as children's or youth work, questions about budgets and expenses need to be clarified rather than assumptions being made with consequent difficulties arising.

All this is actually about honouring and valuing people, treating them seriously, ensuring that commensurate support is given to match the expectations we have of volunteers. Again, to quote Steven Croft, it is in fact about helping churches move from 'an ethos of volunteers to an ethos of vocation'.[13]

Frequently I now find myself sitting down with people and asking them: 'What do you enjoy doing? What gives you a buzz?' It is a matter of seeking to align the volunteer's role with their gifts and passions. If these are misplaced it can adversely affect not only the person's life, but also the life of the church. So if they are a 'people person', in what direction might their service work out? If they are more a 'systems/organisation person', where might they channel their energies? If we ask these and related questions, people will realise that the leader cares and is more concerned that people enjoy and are fulfilled in their area of service, than simply that a particular post is filled. The chances are that the more people are working in areas in which they enjoy themselves and in which they find fulfilment, the better will be the work that they do. It will also help them to persist and persevere when things are difficult. Do we sometimes miss this basic ingredient?

In addition to what has gone before, I would add four final insights into this crucial, yet easily overlooked area:

- *Help and training in the language used* would help many clergy and churches. As an example of this, the NCV (National Council for Volunteering) strapline for recruiting people in the Millennium year was 'Build on what you're into' – seeing volunteering as an extension of what people are committed to and doing anyway, rather than as an add-on.

- *Learning to see and promote volunteering as an 'exchange' relationship* – the church benefits but there are clear benefits to the volunteers themselves. It is not one-way traffic.

- *Avoid soft-pedalling* in terms of what is expected of volunteers, but equally do not make undue or unrealistic demands either. Remember they have a life, a career and a family beyond their church involvement. Putting oneself forward can be quite daunting, and it can be useful to offer 'tasters' of an area of service or ministry, so the new volunteer and others involved can get to know one another and see whether this is the right niche.

- *Endings are important.* Enabling people to relinquish or lay down a task when the time is right, with appreciation in writing as well as expressed verbally, is a demonstration of respect. In my mind this applies whether the person has been carrying out the task for one year or twenty-five years, whether it has been a high-profile responsibility or very much behind the scenes.

Building some of these strategies into the ways we go about seeking volunteers will not solve all the Church's recruitment problems overnight. Nevertheless, when more thought is given to some of the principles outlined, linking volunteering to vocation, it will perhaps help people to grasp that what we are asking them to do is a significant task and worth giving time and energy to. Indeed research has shown that most people who don't currently volunteer say they would if approached – it seems it is all a question of how they are approached, and what support and accountability is in place.

Supervision skills

Looking, as we have been, at working with and supporting volunteers, it follows that some of those volunteers will be fulfilling key roles that require a level of formal supervision. These include, for example, readers or lay preachers, lay evangelists, worship leaders, administrators, youth and children's workers, pastoral assistants. In some situations these may be paid posts and, of course, some clergy have curates or assistant ministers for whom they have supervisory responsibilities. From my own experience and research on the ground, it seems that clergy often do not take their supervisory responsibilities seriously, nor have they received training to develop the key skills necessary.

At the age of thirty, with only the experience of being a curate myself to help, I was asked to take on a deaconess, out of college, with the recognition that this was a training post. Similarly, three years later I was asked to take on a male curate, also straight out of college. Happily, I had enjoyed a positive experience as a curate with a wonderful and experienced training incumbent, as the Church of England calls them. But as I came to have supervisory and training responsibilities myself, all I had to fall back on was his example, because no one suggested any training or other resources. Basically, we had to learn as we went along.

Nowadays, some dioceses at least are making it compulsory that anyone who has a training responsibility must have completed some kind of supervision skills course. This is long overdue, and in my judgement should be compulsory in every diocese or the equivalent in other denominations.

What exactly is meant by supervision? There are essentially three possible ways of interpreting a supervisory role, reflecting different kinds of needs and situations. First, there is *line management supervision* – the proper exercise of accountability to a management figure with responsibility for the oversight of the work as a whole. Here the focus is on ensuring that the work gets done. It can be carried out in a variety of ways, including ongoing or ad hoc contact in the course of the work, as well as regular more formal meetings.

At the other end of the spectrum, a supervisor may find themselves from time to time in a *support* or counselling role, where the aim is to help the worker to feel and think through the pressures that are affecting them, arising from their work or from life in general, and to recognise successes and achievements. Here the focus is on the person rather than the task or the work. This may be necessary if a crisis arises, but also is something I would explore with paid staff on an occasional basis, say two or three times a year, as part of the process of ongoing training, reflection and review.

Third, there is *non-managerial supervision*. This assumes a different kind of relationship, more to do with a co-operative process of discussing work regularly, with the focus on 'self as an effective worker'. This normally operates on the basis of regular, confidential and uninterrupted meetings of an agreed length – usually between one and two hours, at fortnightly or monthly intervals. Supervision of this kind, aimed at furthering professional competence, developing skills and personal awareness, is distinguished from counselling in that the aim is to support the work rather than the supervised person per se.

It seems to me that the kind of supervision clergy are involved in, particularly as far as paid staff are concerned, is a combination of all of these. There are certain parallels here to some models of social work provision. Thus, Parsloe and Hill[14] consider there are two major purposes to supervision:

(1) to establish the accountability of the worker to the organisation;
(2) to promote the worker's development as a professional person.

They go on to state that 'since accountability is concerned not only with whether a task is performed but also with the quality or standard of the work, the two purposes of supervision are practically and conceptually interwoven.' Certainly, the fortnightly supervision sessions I hold with my curate and youth worker reflect this mix.

An editorial in *Contact 121* includes the following:

> Supervision offers the worker the opportunity to stand back, reflect and have her own needs met. This checks negative responses, such as scapegoating individuals or groups, and helps to identify new possibilities. The supervised person is supported and so better able to support others without yielding to unrealistic messianism or hopelessness. Supervision provides care for the individual as well as opportunities for self-development, self-awareness and commitment to learning. The supervision process permits the integration of new and old experiences and assumptions. In an ecclesiastical context, it enables the integration of theory, theology and practice which can otherwise easily be compartmentalised. Some kind of supervision is necessary if dysfunctional habits are not to be learned, perpetuated and disseminated. Ideally, supervision can be a kind of learning,

creative "play" in an honest environment where the pressures of work can be felt, explored and understood and ways forward discerned. It is one of the few ways of preventing burnout. It counters the kind of disillusion that leads to the suspicion that some ministers are experienced only in that they have survived years of having the same year's experience over and over again, becoming inured to the real needs of others and to new possibilities en route. Without supervision, people perish. Worse still, future generations inherit this baleful legacy.[15]

What then might the ingredients of a supervision skills course include? Key areas would seem to be:

- understanding the supervision process;
- exploring how adults learn;
- identifying and practising the practical skills of supervision;
- examining issues of power and authority, and working with difference;
- proposing guidelines for good practice;
- developing strategies for tackling poor performance.

It seems to me that supervision and support are essential for anyone wanting to work effectively with people. This is why it has long been recognised in the police and prison services, social and probation work and other support agencies, teaching, medical staff and counsellors. Evidence seems to show that where structures for support and commitment to such values are in place, the informal culture becomes more supportive.

Not only is this about clergy learning to offer supervision to those for whom they are responsible; it also raises the question of 'who supervises the supervisors?' The Revd David Charles-Edwards, a management consultant and part-time stipendiary priest, who has worked both in secular and church contexts, would argue that, as people involved in dealing regularly with serious and demanding pastoral situations, clergy should have professional supervision every six to eight weeks to provide a necessary mix of support and challenge. The Diocese of Lichfield has been exploring the possibility of providing this facility. In a pilot study in two Anglican deaneries, clergy have had access to this kind of professional supervision at that frequency for one-and-a-half hours at a time. On an ongoing basis, such support would of course have financial implications – but if, as Andrew Irvine states, 'the clergy are the church's most significant asset',[16] can we afford *not* to provide such support and challenge?

In the final section of the draft *Guidelines for the Professional Conduct of the Clergy* this is echoed in two places.

> Where some form of work consultancy is available, it should be offered by trained personnel whose work is monitored and reviewed by the appropriate officers.[17]

> The Bishop and those exercising pastoral care of the clergy should, both by word and example, actively encourage the clergy to adopt a healthy lifestyle. This should include adequate time for leisure, through taking days off and their full holiday entitlement, developing interests outside their main area of ministry and maintaining a commitment to the care and development of themselves and their personal relationships. Helping the clergy understand and overcome unrealistic expectations within themselves and from the outside world needs to be a priority.[18]

8
Epilogue: time and choice

I n this book I have tried to describe something of the impact of a changing world on Christian leaders and identify some possible strategies for sustaining an effective ministry. If you find yourself agreeing with at least some of the analysis, you might nonetheless feel somewhat overwhelmed. Indeed as I have been writing I have thought more than once of that phrase, 'Physician, heal thyself.' (I have even considered giving the book a fresh title such as 'Fit for What?'!)

One possible response to that sense of being overwhelmed by all that is changing around us is to settle for a level of mediocrity – lives marked more by survival than sustenance. It seems that our world has become the world of the Red Queen in Lewis Carroll's *Through the Looking-Glass*: 'Now, *here*, you see, it takes all the running *you* can do to keep in the same place. If you want to get somewhere else, you must run at least twice as fast as that!'[1]

So you may find yourself thinking:

- 'I'd love to start keeping that spiritual journal but . . .'
- 'I know I ought to take more exercise and eat more healthily, but . . .'
- 'I must go on an annual CME course but . . .'
- 'I must find a spiritual director but . . .'
- 'I must block out more time for family and friends, but . . .'

I haven't got time!

Although this is now the twenty-first century, as long ago as the 1950s, the French Roman Catholic priest and writer Michel Quoist captured this sense of not having enough time for what is really important. In *Prayers of Life*, he writes: 'All men complain that they haven't enough time. It's because they look at their lives from too human a point of view. There's always time to do what God wants us to do, but we must put ourselves completely into each moment that he offers us.'[2]

These thoughts are then encapsulated in a prayer, 'Lord, I have time', which concludes with these words:

But we must not lose time
                waste time
                kill time
For time is a gift that you give us,
But a perishable gift,
A gift that does not keep.

Lord, I have time,
I have plenty of time,
All the time that you give me,
The years of my life,
The days of my years,
The hours of my days,
They are all mine.
Mine to fill, quietly, calmly,
But to fill completely, up to the brim,
To offer them to you, that of their insipid water
You may make a rich wine such as you made once in Cana
        of Galilee.

I am not asking you tonight, Lord, for time to do this and
        then that,
But your grace to do conscientiously, in the time that you
        give me, what you want me to do.

In Chapter 3, 'Taking care of ourselves', I gave some practical pointers as to how time might be better used for the well-being of the minister. Building on that, what I believe is needed for things to be different is a fresh understanding in two areas – *the rhythm of life* and *the gift of choice*. Few clergy today (I imagine!) are like the one I heard of, who, when being paid a surprise visit by his archdeacon, said: 'How nice to see you. I was wondering what to do this afternoon.' He could be commended for his honesty, but his understanding of the use of time left something to be desired! I am not suggesting a secular, performance-based approach to ministry, which would contradict much of what I have written about earlier. I believe most clergy work hard, but I have come to understand that working hard is not necessarily the same as working effectively and strategically. There are external pressures and expectations on clergy that are different from, and arguably greater than in previous generations, but there is a need for clergy to beware getting into a kind of victim mode.

The rhythm of life

Although the clock is a Chinese invention, used from around AD 500, it only began to assume prominence in the western world in the late seventeenth century. When timepieces appeared, they brought massive ideological changes with them. For those who possessed or had access to them, they were a means of power, for they could now begin to have notions of efficient use of time. At the same time, the regularity and systems that clocks introduced also brought with them a sense of inhumanity. They reflected a change of ethos from seeing time as unlimited. Until then, time had been measured in the natural rhythms of days and seasons coming round again as in a circle. Clocks introduced a way of seeing time as linear, each moment a unique opportunity, limited and unrepeatable. The Protestant work ethic emerged out of this way of seeing time, concerned always to 'redeem the time', with a wise stewardship of God's resources, including time.

It is important not to lose the positive and healthy sense that time is a gift from God to be stewarded and not squandered. Looking back to the Old Testament Scriptures we see it was the rhythm of the festivals and seasons that helped to shape life for the Hebrew people. When the psalmist was under pressure on one occasion he wrote: 'The day is yours, and yours also the night; you established the sun and moon ... you made both summer and winter' (Psalm 74:16–17). The constant return of seedtime and harvest may still have something to teach us.

In giving practical contemporary expression to this, I am indebted to my friend, Robin Gamble, who is currently Canon Missioner in Manchester Diocese. During a residential conference for clergy on the subject of using our time, he pointed out that both for the health and well-being of the clergy and church members, seasons of activity need to be followed by 'fallow' time. 'Too often,' he said, 'clergy and churches just go on accumulating tasks, and there is no sense of ebb and flow.' To avoid this, good planning is needed, which comes more naturally to some than others! If clergy worked with their local lay leaders to see what this might look like in their context, it could prevent an experience of church life that is marked either by dull predictability or frenetic activity. Either of these is sapping for clergy and church members alike. The seasons of the year and of the Church's year can remind us how activity followed by withdrawal can provide a healthy rhythm for life and ministry.

David Runcorn writes: 'The natural world around us has its seasons. There is light and darkness, winter and summer, dryness and fruitfulness. So it is with the Christian life. And unless we understand that there are seasons of faith in the heart also, we will tend to be very hard on ourselves. We will always be trying to maintain a peak of confident faith and victorious living. We will be living with an ideal.'[3]

The gift of choice

Having this kind of understanding of time and life might bring much-needed perspective on a healthier and more sustainable ministry. David Runcorn has this to say about what can feel to be the 'tyranny of time': 'I must change the question I keep challenging myself with. I cannot just ask, "How should I spend my time?" I must also ask, "Who am I spending my time becoming?" I will not glorify God in my life by doing some *thing – but by becoming someone.'*⁴*

Reading that certainly challenged me. As Thomas Merton put it: 'The Christian does not need to consider time an enemy. Time is not standing between him and anything he desires.'⁵

Even if we do not see time as 'the enemy' and we construe ministry as being more about 'who I am becoming' rather than 'what I achieve', nevertheless we have only got so much emotional, physical and intellectual stamina and only so much time at our disposal. This means we are called upon to make choices. (Remember that 'choice' is a key value in these post-modern times!) The choices we make as to how our time and energy are invested will be determined by a number of factors. These will include personality, gifting, personal circumstances and current context for ministry.

Illustrating this from personal experience, I am not a particularly technologically orientated person. (People who know me well would say that was a gross understatement!) Some people love nothing more than keeping up with the latest developments and possibilities in IT. For me, that is not time well spent. I am a 'people person', with the strong conviction, evident throughout this book, that ministry is fundamentally relational, and I enjoy nothing more as a leader than seeing people developing their full potential. However, I recognise the importance of technology and its potential for the Church's ministry in the twenty-first century. Thus, in the church for which I am currently responsible, the church office has e-mail facilities, there is a church web site, and we are in process of installing video-projection facilities and TV monitors in the church building. This arises not from a desire to ape the world, but from our passion as a church to discover more visual and creative ways to communicate the Christian faith and enable encounter with God. We recognise that, these days, electronic communication is a significant means by which people receive and process information and experience the world.

I see my task in this not as getting involved 'hands on' with new technology but, as a leader, sharing the vision for these new possibilities and encouraging and supporting others, who do have the appropriate skills and interests to deliver what is needed. What matters is that those called into leadership know themselves, cultivate and develop their own gifting and ensure that where they are weak, they compensate for this by encouraging and developing others in such areas.

This may sound too idealistic. You may be tempted to think that in the larger church situation in which I work, it is somehow easier to operate in this way. My response would be that I have also sought to apply these principles in an urban priority area and a rural setting. Of course I have to say that after nearly thirty years of ordained ministry, mainly as a 'GP' in local church situations, I know we have at times to be ready to turn our hands to anything. We may on occasions feel overwhelmed by the many different demands of ministry. The other side of the coin is the privilege of the variety of the ministerial task. Flexibility, as I have commented earlier, is also a gift to be valued.

But I return to the principle stated earlier, that a fundamental task for leaders is to know their own strengths and to help those for whom they are responsible to know and develop theirs. This is not a matter of discarding tasks that are uncongenial, but asking: 'Could X do this, and do it more effectively, than me?'

Once again, we face what are, I believe, theological principles. 'Taking responsibility for ourselves' includes making good choices about how and where time and energy are invested, and reflecting on whether we are becoming more the people God created us to be. The secret of Jesus' choices and priorities being the 'right' ones came out of the freedom with which he lived. That in turn came from his life on earth being sustained by the life of heaven. He lived in time, but took his priorities from eternity. 'That is why unlike us he always "had time" for life, and gave each moment his full attention.'[6]

These are demanding and challenging times in which to be

involved in leadership in the Church. Constant change really is here to stay! But I believe they are also times of opportunity. This is why I feel profoundly sad when at local church, diocesan or national levels, survival and cutbacks seem to be the name of the game. What is needed is fresh vision of an emerging environment that embodies hope. We are in unfamiliar territory in many ways and surely dare not draw back in search of some elusive, long-gone safety and security. Rather, I would echo Michael Riddell's words: 'The new millennium is a time for irresponsible boldness.'[7]

It is the clergy who need to be at the forefront of such boldness, well resourced and trained and appropriately affirmed and valued.

Notes

Chapter 1:
Taking the temperature – the context for ministry at the beginning of the twenty-first century

1 Ian Bunting, *Models of Ministry* (Grove Books, 1994), p. 3.
2 Michael Moynagh, 'Church 2020 – what will it be like?' in *RUN* magazine (Spring 1999), p. 9.
3 John Finney, *Recovering the Past* (Darton, Longman & Todd, 1996), p. 1.
4 Michael Nazir-Ali, *Shapes of the Church to Come* (Kingsway, 2001), p. 196.
5 John Drane, 'Was God in Dunblane?', as published in *Baptist Times* (21 March 1996), p. 8.
6 J. W. Fowler, *Faithful Change* (Abingdon Press, 1996), p. 147.
7 S. Grenz, *A Primer on Postmodernism* (Eerdmans, 1996).
8 Graham Cray, *Youth Congregations and the Emerging Church* (Grove Books, 2002), p. 9.
9 Robert Warren, *Being Human, Being Church* (Marshall Pickering, 1995), p. 34.
10 Grace Davie, *Religion in Britain since 1945: Believing without Belonging* (Blackwell, 1994).
11 John Finney, *Finding Faith Today* (Bible Society, 1992).
12 H. Knight III, *A Future for Truth* (Abingdon Press, 1997), p. 68.
13 Mick Brown, *The Spiritual Tourist*, quoted in David Lewis and Darren Bridger, *The Soul of the New Consumer* (Nicholas Brealey, 2001).
14 John Finney, *Recovering the Past* (Darton, Longman & Todd, 1996).
15 Stuart Murray, 'A decade of experimentation – redesigning the Church for post-Christendom' in *The Bible in Transmission* (Bible Society, Summer 2001).

Chapter 2:
Identity and morale
1 John Adair, in Nelson John (ed.), *Leading, Managing and Ministering* (Canterbury Press, 1999), p. viii.
2 Mary Anne Coate, *Clergy Stress* (SPCK, 1989), p. 14.
3 John Sandford, *Ministry Burnout* (Arthur James Ltd, 1982), pp. 5–15.
4 Andrew Clitherow, *Into Your Hands* (SPCK, 2001), p. 65.

Chapter 3:
Taking care of ourselves
1 Gregory the Great, *Pastoral Rule*, Part IV, I.
2 John Chrysostom, *On the Priesthood*, VI, 10, 16.
3 Andrew Irvine, *Between Two Worlds* (Mowbray, 1997), pp. 107 and 110.
4 Henri Nouwen, *The Way of the Heart* (Darton, Longman & Todd, 1981), p. 31.
5 Lesslie Newbigin, *The Gospel in a Pluralist Society* (SPCK, 1989), pp. 240–1.
6 Michael Riddell, *Threshold of the Future* (SPCK, 1998), p. 143.
7 Richard Foster, *Prayer* (Hodder & Stoughton, 1992), p. 273.
8 Henri Nouwen, *The Way of the Heart*, p. 20.
9 Thomas Merton, *The Asian Journal* (Sheldon Press, 1974).
10 Henri Nouwen, *The Genesee Diary: Report from a Trappist Monastery* (Doubleday, 1976).
11 Henri Nouwen, *The Genesee Diary*, p. 160.
12 Quoted in Eric James, *A life of Bishop John A. T. Robinson: Scholar, Pastor, Prophet* (Collins, 1987), p. 285.
13 Lawrence Osborn, *Dear Diary – An Introduction to Spiritual Journalling* (Grove, 1988), p. 4.
14 Lawrence Osborn, *Dear Diary*, p. 7.
15 *The Alternative Service Book 1980* (Mowbray, 1980), p. 373.
16 J. R. W. Stott, *I Believe in Preaching* (Hodder & Stoughton, 1982).
17 Sarah Horsman, *Living with Stress – A Guide for Ministers and Church Leaders* (Lutterworth Press, 1989), p. 87.
18 Sarah Horsman, *Living with Stress*, pp. 88–90.
19 David Fisher, *The 21st Century Pastor* (Zondervan, 1996) quoted in *Netfax 49, The Leadership Network*, 8 July 1996, *http://www.leadnet.org.*
20 Gerard Kelly, *Get a Grip on the Future without Losing Your Hold on the Past* (Monarch, 1999) p. 246.
21 Henri Nouwen, *In the Name of Jesus* (Darton, Longman & Todd, 2000), p. 50.

22 Stephen R. Covey and A. Roger Merrill, *First Things First* (Simon & Schuster, 1994).

23 Bill Hybels, 'The art of self-leadership' in *Leadership* magazine, Summer 2001.

24 Henri Nouwen, *In the Name of Jesus*, p. 30.

25 Mary Anne Coate, *Clergy Stress* (SPCK, 1989), p. 198.

26 Alan Bennett, *Telling Tales* (BBC Books, 2000).

Chapter 4:
The nearest and dearest

1 Mary Anne Coate, *Clergy Stress* (SPCK, 1989), p. 80.

2 Andrew Clitherow, *Into Your Hands* (SPCK, 2001), p. 62.

3 Wanda Nash, *Living with God at the Vicarage* (Grove Books, 1990), p. 5.

4 Andrew Irvine, *Between Two Worlds: Understanding and Managing Clergy Stress* (Mowbray, 1997), p. 139.

5 R. J. Pryor, *At Cross Purposes: Stress and Support in the Ministry of the Wounded Healer* (The Commission on Continuing Education for Ministry, Uniting Church in Australia, Synod of Victoria, 1986).

6 Andrew Irvine, *Between Two Worlds*, pp. 140–1.

7 Society of Martha and Mary, Sheldon, Dunsford, Exeter EX6 7LE.

8 John Sandford, *Ministry Burnout* (Arthur James Books Ltd, 1982), p. 19.

9 Andrew Irvine, *Between Two Worlds*, p. 83.

10 Sarah Meyrick, *Married to the Ministry* (Triangle, 1998), p. 134.

11 Sarah Meyrick, *Married to the Ministry*, p. 12.

12 Terry Lovell, *Number One* (HarperCollins, 1997), p. 12.

13 Sarah Meyrick, *Married to the Ministry*, p. 46.

Chapter 5:
Who cares for the carers?

1 Christopher Spence, *On Watch* (Cassell, 1996).

2 Nancy Kline, *Time to Think* (Ward Lock, 1999).

3 Nancy Kline, *Time to Think*, p. 13.

4 Nancy Kline, *Time to Think*, p. 13.

5 Steven Croft, *Ministry in Three Dimensions* (Darton, Longman & Todd, 1999).

6 Andrew Irvine, *Between Two Worlds: Understanding and Managing Clergy Stress* (Mowbray, 1997), pp. 160–79.

7 Diocese of Carlisle, *Handbook for Church Councils*.

8 Barbara Gilbert, *Who Ministers to Ministers?* (The Alban Institute, 1987), p. 1.

9 Shirley Hodgson, *Spiritual Guidance* (Mowbray, 1954), p. 3.

10 Margaret Guenther, *Holy Listening* (Darton, Longman & Todd, 1992).

Chapter 6:
Tools for the trade: personal development

1 *Draft Document: Guidelines for the Professional Conduct of the Clergy* (February 2002), Section 6:3.

2 Gerard Kelly, *Get a Grip on the Future without Losing Your Hold on the Past* (Monarch, 1999), p. 245.

3 Archbishops' Council, *Mind the Gap – Integrated Continuing Ministerial Education for the Church's Ministers* (Church House Publishing, 2001).

4 *Mind the Gap*, p. 20.

5 John Reader, *Local Theology* (SPCK, 1994).

6 Robert Warren, *Being Human, Being Church* (Marshall Pickering, 1995), p. 80.

7 *The Alternative Service Book 1980*, p. 356.

8 Diocese of Rochester, *Ministry Review Handbook*, June 1999.

9 *Draft Document*, Part II:12:8.

10 Rochester *Ministry Review Handbook*.

11 Archbishops' Council, *Mind the Gap*, p. 77.

12 Andrew Irvine, *Between Two Worlds: Understanding and Managing Clergy Stress* (Mowbray, 1997), p. 165.

13 Archbishops' Council, *Mind the Gap*, pp. 77–8.

14 Wanda Nash, *At Ease with Stress* (Darton, Longman & Todd, 1988).

Chapter 7:
Tools for the trade: ministerial skills

1 John Adair, *The Leadership of Jesus and its Legacy Today* (Canterbury Press, 2001), p. 109.

2 *The Report of the Working Party on Criteria for Selection for Ministry in the Church of England*, ABM Policy Paper No. 3A (October 1993), p. 102, quoted in Steven Croft, *Ministry in Three Dimensions* (Darton, Longman & Todd, 1999), p. 14.

3 John Finney, *Understanding Leadership* (Daybreak/Darton, Longman & Todd, 1989), p. 84.

4 John Adair, *Action Centred Leadership* (Ashgate,1979).

5 Bryn Hughes, *Leadership Tool Kit* (Monarch, 1998), p. 194.

6 John Finney, *Understanding Leadership*.

7 Anglican Church of Canada press statement (2000).

8 David Cormack, *Change Directions* (Monarch, 1995), p. 162.

9 Everett Rodgers, *Diffusion of Innovations* (Simon & Schuster, 1995).

10 Heard at the Willow Creek 'Prevailing Churches' Conference in 1997.

11 National Centre for Volunteering, *The Recruitment Guide* (1999).

12 Steven Croft, *Ministry in Three Dimensions*, p. 176.

13 Steven Croft, *Ministry in Three Dimensions*, p. 176.

14 Parsloe and Hill, DHSS document (1978).

15 *Contact 121*, Editorial (1996).

16 Andrew Irvine, *Between Two Worlds: Understanding and Managing Clergy Stress* (Mowbray, 1997), p. 163.

17 Archbishops' Council, *Draft Document: Guidelines for the Professional Conduct of Clergy,* Section 12:9.

18 *Draft Document*, Section 12:14.

Chapter 8:
Epilogue: time and choice

1 Lewis Carroll, *Through the Looking-Glass* (1872), Ch. 2.

2 Michel Quoist, *Prayers of Life* (Gill & Macmillan, English translation 1964), p. 76.

3 David Runcorn, from the chapter 'Time to be' in Derek Williams (ed.), *Time to Live* (Triangle, 1987), p. 133.

4 David Runcorn, 'Time to be', p. 123.

5 Thomas Merton, *Seasons of Celebration* (Farrer, Straus & Giroux, 1977), p. 48.

6 David Runcorn, 'Time to Be', p. 126.

7 Michael Riddell, *Threshold of the Future* (SPCK,1998), p. 117.

Select bibliography

The scriptural quotations are taken from the *The Holy Bible, New International Version*, unless otherwise stated.

Adair, John, *Action Centred Leadership*, Ashgate, 1979.

Adair, John, *The Leadership of Jesus and its Legacy Today*, Canterbury Press, 2001.

Anderson, Ray, *The Soul of Ministry*, Westminster John Knox Press, 1997.

Archbishops' Council, *Generosity and Sacrifice – the Report of the Clergy Stipends Review Group*, Church House Publishing, 2001.

Archbishops' Council, *Mind the Gap – Integrated Continuing Ministerial Education for the Church's Ministers*, Church House Publishing, 2001.

Atkins, Martyn D., *Preaching in a Cultural Context*, Foundery Press, 2001.

Berger, Peter, *The Desecularization of the World*, Eerdmans, 1999.

Brierley, Peter, *Vision Building*, Hodder & Stoughton, 1989.

Brown, Callum G., *The Death of Christian Britain*, Routledge, 2001.

Bunting, Ian, *Models of Ministry*, Grove Books, 1994.

Clitherow, Andrew, *Into Your Hands*, SPCK, 2001.

Coate, Mary Anne, *Clergy Stress*, SPCK, 1989.

Cormack, David, *Change Directions*, Monarch, 1995.

Coupland, Douglas, *Generation X*, St Martin's Press, 1991.

Covey, Stephen R., *The Seven Habits of Highly Effective People*, Simon & Schuster, 1990.

Covey, Stephen R. and Merrill, A. Roger, *First Things First*, Simon & Schuster, 1994.

Cray, Graham, *Youth Congregations and the Emerging Church*, Grove Books, 2002.

Croft, Steven, *Ministry in Three Dimensions*, Darton, Longman & Todd, 1999.

Davey, John, *Burn Out: Stress in the Ministry*, Gracewing, 1995.

Davie, Grace, *Religion in Britain since 1945: Believing without Belonging*, Blackwell, 1994.

Dewar, Francis, *Live for a Change*, Darton, Longman & Todd, 1988.

Dewar, Francis, *Called or Collared? An Alternative Approach to Vocation*, SPCK, 1991.

Drane, John, *Cultural Change and Biblical Faith*, Paternoster Press, 2000.

Drane, John, *The McDonaldization of the Church*, Darton, Longman & Todd, 2000.

Eastell, Kevin (ed.), *Appointed for Growth: A Handbook of Ministry Development and Appraisal*, Mowbray, 1994.

Edmondson, Chris, *Strategies for Rural Evangelism*, Grove Books, 1989.

Edmondson, Chris, *How Shall They Hear?*, Grove Books, 1994.

Edmondson, Chris, *Minister – Love Thyself*, Grove Books, 2000.

Finney, John, *Understanding Leadership*, Daybreak/Darton, Longman & Todd, 1989.

Finney, John, *Church on the Move*, Daybreak/Darton, Longman & Todd, 1992.

Finney, John, *Finding Faith Today*, Bible Society, 1992.

Finney, John, *Recovering the Past*, Darton, Longman & Todd, 1996.

Foster, Richard, *Prayer*, Hodder & Stoughton, 1992.

Foskett, John and Lyall, David, *Helping the Helpers: Supervision and Pastoral Care*, SPCK, 1988.

Fowke, Ruth, *Personality and Prayer*, Eagle, 1997.

Fowler, J. W., *Faithful Change*, Abingdon Press, 1996.

Francis, Leslie J. and Richter, Philip, *Gone but not Forgotten*, Darton, Longman & Todd, 1988.

Gamble, Robin, *The Irrelevant Church*, Monarch, 1991.

Gibbs, Eddie, *Followed or Pushed?*, Marc Europe, 1987.

Gilbert, Barbara, *Who Ministers to Ministers?*, Alban Institute, 1987.

Goldsmith, Malcolm, *Knowing Me, Knowing God*, Triangle, 1994.

Greenwood, Robin, *Reclaiming the Church*, Fount, 1988.

Greenwood, Robin, *Transforming Priesthood*, SPCK, 1994.

Grenz, S., *A Primer on Postmodernism*, Eerdmans, 1996.

Grundy, Malcolm, *Understanding Congregations*, Mowbray, 1998.

Guenther, Margaret, *Holy Listening*, Darton, Longman & Todd, 1992.

Hodgson, Shirley, *Spiritual Guidance*, Mowbray, 1954.

Horsman, Sarah, *Living with Stress*, Lutterworth Press, 1989.

Hughes, Bryn, *Leadership Tool Kit*, Monarch, 1998.

Hybels, Lynne and Bill, *Rediscovering Church*, HarperCollins, 1996.

Irvine, Andrew, *Between Two Worlds: Understanding and Managing Clergy Stress*, Mowbray, 1997.

Kay, William, *Personality and Renewal*, Grove Books, 2001.

Kelly, Gerard, *Get a Grip on the Future without Losing Your Hold on the Past*, Monarch, 1999.

Kline, Nancy, *Time To Think*, Ward Lock, 1999.

Knight III, H., *A Future for Truth*, Abingdon Press, 1997.

Lewis, David and Bridger, Darren, *The Soul of the New Consumer*, Nicholas Brealey, 2001.

MacDonald, Gordon, *Ordering Your Private World*, Highland, 1984.

Merton, Thomas, *The Asian Journal*, Sheldon Press, 1974.

Meyrick, Sarah, *Married to the Ministry*, Triangle, 1998.

Mitton, Michael, *Restoring the Woven Chord*, Darton, Longman & Todd, 1995.

Moynagh, Michael, *Changing World, Changing Church*, Monarch, 2001.

Nash, Wanda, *At Ease with Stress*, Darton, Longman & Todd, 1988.

Nash, Wanda, *Living with God at the Vicarage*, Grove Books, 1990.

Nash, Wanda, *Christ, Stress and Glory*, Darton, Longman & Todd, 1997.

Nazir-Ali, Michael, *Shapes of the Church to Come*, Kingsway, 2001.

Nelson, John (ed.), *Management and Ministry*, Canterbury Press, 1996.

Nelson, John (ed.), *Leading, Managing and Ministering*, Canterbury Press, 1999.

Newbigin, Lesslie, *The Gospel in a Pluralist Society*, SPCK, 1989.

Nouwen, Henri, *The Way of the Heart*, Darton, Longman & Todd, 1981.

Nouwen, Henri, *In the Name of Jesus*, Darton, Longman & Todd, 2000.

Quoist, Michel, *Prayers of Life*, English translation Gill & Macmillan, 1963.

Reader, John, *Local Theology*, SPCK, 1994.

Riddell, Michael, *Threshold of the Future*, SPCK, 1998.

Riddell, Michael, *Sacred Journey*, Lion, 2000.

Robinson, Martin, *The Faith of the Unbeliever*, Monarch, 1994.

Rodgers, Everett, *Diffusion of Innovations*, Simon & Schuster, 1995.

Sampson, Philip, Samuel, Vinay and Sudgen, Chris, *Faith and Modernity*, Regnum Books, 1992.

Sandford, John, *Ministry Burnout*, Arthur James Books Ltd, 1982.

Senge, Peter M., *The Fifth Discipline: The Art and Practice of the Learning Organization*, Doubleday/Currency Books, 1990.

Simpson, Ray, *Soul Friendship*, Hodder & Stoughton, 1999.

Spence, Christopher, *On Watch*, Cassell, 1996.

Taylor, James, *Pastors under Pressure*, Day One, 2001.

Thornton, Martin, *Spiritual Direction*, SPCK, 1984.

Tiller, John, *The Gospel Community and its Leadership*, Marshall Pickering, 1987.

Wagner, Peter, *Leading Your Church to Growth*, Marc Europe, 1984.

Walker, Andrew, *Telling the Story: Gospel, Mission and Culture*, SPCK, 1996.

Warren, Robert, *On the Anvil*, Highland, 1990.

Warren, Robert, *Being Human, Being Church*, Marshall Pickering, 1995.

Warren, Robert, *Building Missionary Congregations*, Church House Publishing, 1995.

Williams, Derek (ed.), *Time to Live*, Triangle, 1987.